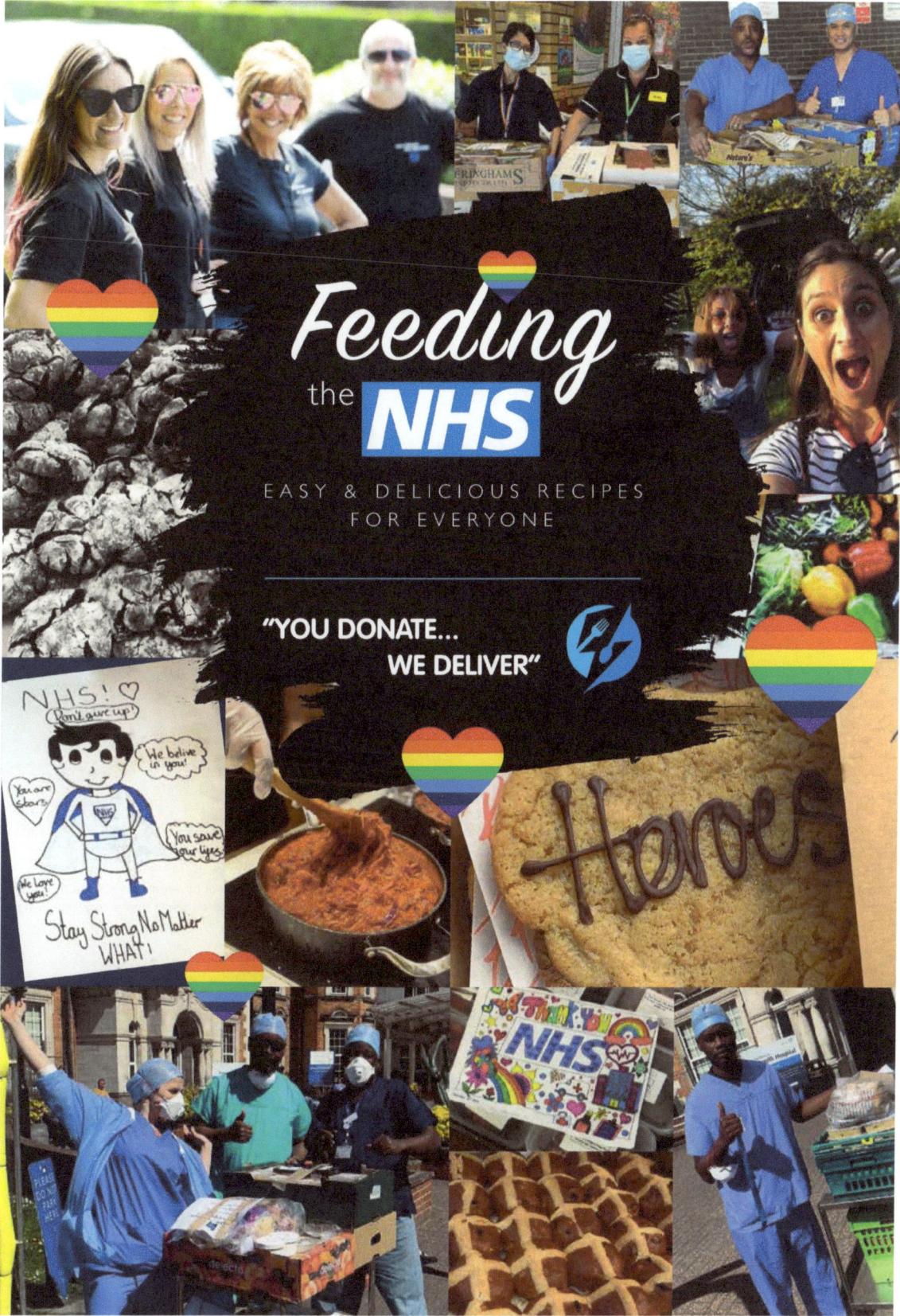

Published by New Generation Publishing in 2020

Copyright © Marc Trainis 2020

First Edition

The author asserts the moral right under the Copyright, Designs and Patents Act 1988 to be identified as the author of this work.

All Rights reserved. No part of this publication may be reproduced, stored in a retrieval system or transmitted, in any form or by any means without the prior consent of the author, nor be otherwise circulated in any form of binding or cover other than that which it is published and without a similar condition being imposed on the subsequent purchaser.

ISBN: 978-1-80031-680-5

www.newgeneration-publishing.com

New Generation Publishing

This book is dedicated to the thousands of frontline NHS workers who are fighting this battle against Corona Virus, showing care, compassion and dedication to their work...

We L♥VE YOU ALL...

Foreword by Marc Trainis

'An Army Marches on its Stomach' Napoleon once said...

'You Donate... We Deliver' was borne out of a necessity to feed a couple of departments at a North West London Hospital where the sister of one of the founders of YDWD works as a registrar. It became apparent that getting a good meal when the Covid-19 pandemic exploded in March 2020 was going to be difficult & the thought of shopping after a 16-hour shift, with empty shelves was not an option.

Sarah Laster along with her friend Katie Icklow, Katie's mum Jackie Commissar together with another friend David Benveniste came together & created 'You Donate... We Deliver. Some phone calls to some other friends who are chefs, caterers, home cooks, with David organising drivers & rota's, more & more hospitals on board, more chefs, more drivers, more gazebos on Katie's driveway (every week another one), 500 meals a day, 1000 meals a day & recently over 2000 meals a day & counting. It is an astonishing feat of organisation, community spirit, generous donations of food, equipment, money, time & lots of socially distanced love.

There are literally hundreds of people I could list here & thank, but we don't have the space!! But we do want to thank everyone single person involved in making YDWD what it is from the 4 founders, those who run the other hubs in Bushey, St Albans, Hampstead Garden Suburb, Totteridge, Mill Hill, Stanmore, Kings Langley, Radlett & Borehamwood, the drivers, the suppliers, the amazing chefs, cooks & caterers, who's incredible food, cakes, biscuits we get the pleasure of delivering & putting smiles on faces of those that most need it.. Our NHS Heroes...

Whilst this cookery book is ultimately for them, it is also for every one of us in the UK to say thank you...

From all of us at YDWD... THANK YOU NHS WORKERS, WE LOVE YOU ALL...

Every penny raised from the sale of this book will go to 'You Donate... We Deliver'

To donate directly please visit:
https://www.gofundme.com/f/UDonateWeDeliver

Front & Rear covers designed by Jo Eden – October Design

INDEX TO CHEFS & RECIPES

Page	Chef	Recipe
4	Foreword	
6	Abbi Rozentals	Moroccan Chicken
7-8	Alessandro Colli	Homemade Pesto with Pasta | Pasta alla Puttanesca
9	Alison Rodol	Mac 'n' Cheese with Broccoli & Peas
10	Ana Martin	Sugar Cookies
11	Benji Nathan	Benji's Bakes Versatile Cookies
12-13	Beverley Szczech	Veggie Chilli | Tea Loaf | Banana Muffins
15-17	Charlie D'Lima	Wild Focaccia Bread | Vegetarian Thai Green Curry | Sticky Toffee Pudding with Salted Caramel Sauce
18-21	Crave Cakes (Sonal & Alex)	Chocolate & Ginger Cake | Carrot Cake | Rose & Lemon Cupcakes
22	Danine Irwin	Meatballs & Mash
23-25	Debbie Morris	Carrot, Sweet Potato & Coriander Soup | Roasted Vegetables Pasta Bake | Chicken Teriyaki with Rice
26-28	Ellie Raefman	Greek Butterbean Stew | Salmon Teriyaki | Chicken Tikka
29-30	Emma Goldstein	Superfood Salad with Citrus Dressing | Vegetarian Couscous Salad
31	Gillian Jones	Chicken Curry
32-34	Helena Sharpstone	Chicken Casserole | Earl Grey Tea Bread | Microwave Lentil Curry
35-36	Jeanne Wilson	Cheese & Tomato Squares | Spaghetti al Pomodoro
37	John Partridge	'The Jon's Thai Green Chicken Curry'
38-39	Lindsey Jacobs	Rich Spaghetti Bolognaise | Moroccan Vegetable Tagine
40	Madeline Berg	Vegetarian Chilli
41-42	Martine Glass	Salmon Balls | Date Squares
43-45	Natasha Gibbens	Thai Red Curry | The Best Vegan Banana Cake | Banging Vegan Chilli & Couscous
46-48	Penny Beral	Vegetable Curry | Store Cupboard Banana Cake | Risotto NHS
49	Phillipa Bellman	Chicken Tikka Masala NHS
50-52	Renee Yarshon	Pesto Roasted Chicken | Lamb Kofta with Yoghurt Flatbread & Tzatziki | Moroccan Spiced Chicken
53-54	Scott Maslen	'Scott's Shepherd's Pie' (Part I) | 'Scott's Shepherd's Pie' (Part II)
55-57	Shabnam Russo	Lamb Koftas | Chicken Dhansak | Cauliflower with Zahter
58-62	Simone Krieger	Sticky Sesame Chicken | Genovese Penne & Roasted Veg | Sweet & Sour Chicken, Chicken Shawarma
63-66	Tanya Rosenthal	Spinach, Chickpea & Potato Curry | Roasted Veg & Couscous | Oat Choc Chip Cookies | Pret Choc Chip Cookies
67	Victoria Prever	Quinoa, Bulgur Wheat, Cherry Tomato & Herb Salad with Tuna

Chef: Abbi Rozentals

How Did You Get Involved with YDWD?

Hi, my name is Abbi Rozentals & I am a family friend of Katie & Jackie through my wonderful grandma Denise Collins. I first heard about this initiative whilst giving the ladies some wonderful cakes my mum had baked for them & wanted to know how I could help.

As it happens, I have been working for Catering by Penny Beral as a cook for almost three years & I love food! I love to think about it, cook it & eat it & nothing has given me greater pleasure than feeding our wonderful NHS in these strange times. I hope they have enjoyed eating my dish & that those who can now have the recipe will enjoy it too.

It is a special recipe for me as it was one of the first things my husband ever made for me & it was delicious!!

Dish: Moroccan Chicken (Serves 4)

Ingredients:

500g chicken thighs, skinned & boned
500g sweet potatoes, peeled & chopped into small pieces
1 large onion, chopped
1 x 400g tin chopped tomatoes
1 x 400g tin chickpeas, drained
4 cloves of garlic, chopped (you can use 4 tsp of garlic puree/paste)
2 tbsp turmeric
2 tbsp ground coriander
2 tbsp paprika

2 tbsp ginger, grated
2 tbsp ground cumin
2 tbsp smoked paprika
2 tbsp ground ginger
1 orange, juiced (or a glass of orange)
1 cinnamon stick
2 tbsp honey
500ml chicken stock

Directions:

1. Coat chicken in oil & spices, the garlic & season. You can do this the night before to make it extra tasty before cooking the following day
2. Preheat the oven to 150°c
3. Heat a pan with some oil in a casserole dish. Fry the onions until softened then add the chicken & brown on all sides
4. Add the sweet potatoes, honey, chickpeas, chopped tomatoes, orange juice, stock & a stick of cinnamon
5. Put in the oven with a lid on for 1½ - 2 hours
6. If the mixture starts to look a bit too thick add more water

Top Tip – If you prefer the sauce to be reduced more, remove the lid & increase the heat for the last 15 minutes. This really brings out the sweetness in the dish. Serve with plain couscous or flat bread

Chef: Alessandro Colli (Private Chef)

How Did You Get Involved with YDWD?

I am Alessandro Colli from Italy, Alessandria (I'm very proud about my city) & I've been living in London from 7 years I'm private chef & I've been published in Forbes Italy magazine the 24/12/2019 edition.

I'm Private Chef base in London but I have worked around the world including New York & Saudi Arabia where I had my last work experiences. I'm 32 years old & I love my job, I've already collaborated with charities before, I went to India with "Farmacisti in Aiuto" in October 2018 & through a client I have opportunity to do it again, cook for you guys.

I got in contact with the Italian embassy to collect some info about charities that were supporting people in hospitals, Shabnam Russo who introduced me to "You Donate...We Deliver".

I'm very happy to be a part of this group & help people from NHS.

Dish: Homemade Italian Pesto… with Pasta (Serves 4)

Ingredients:

55g of basil leaves (from Italy – Ed. Or somewhere more local!!)
75g Parmigiano Reggiano 36 months
22g pine nuts (toasted)
2 small pinches of salt

100 ml extra virgin olive oil
35g Pecorino Romano
1 cloves garlic

Directions:

1. You need a mortar & pestle for start
2. Let's put basil (don't wash just clean with cloth) & you can add garlic & salt & mix mix in the mortar & pestle
3. When the paste is ready you start with pine nuts & you can add Parmesan & pecorino & you can put slow slow the extra virgin olive oil
4. Your pesto now is ready & you can cook pasta (al dente) & enjoy

Chef: Alessandro Colli

Dish: 'Pasta alla Puttanesca'
(Ed. I was told not to translate this to English as it translates as 'Bitch Pasta!!' who knew?)

Ingredients:

330g of pasta
30g of capers
4 cloves garlic
160g of black olives
45g of extra virgin olive oil

900g of chopped tomato
35g of anchovies
1 bunch of parsley
3 dried chilli
salt & pepper

Directions:

1. You can start with your garlic & olive oil in a large pot & cook a slow heat
2. Then add your olives, chilli & your capers & cook for 4-5 min on a high heat
3. Reduce the heat & add your chopped tomato & cook for at least 45 minutes
4. Turn off the heat & add anchovies mix well & taste for seasoning
5. Add more salt, black pepper if required & finish cooking your spaghetti in the sauce before serving

Enjoy

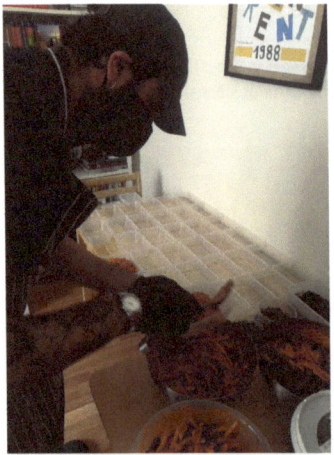

Chef: Alison Rodol

How Did You Get Involved with YDWD?

Usually my days are filled working in Primary Schools & Care Homes helping with cooking sessions which I find immensely rewarding, so naturally when I was contacted during the Covid-19 pandemic it was an easy decision to join the Group & support the NHS as I love to cook & love to help others.

Dish: Mac & Cheese with Broccoli & Peas (Serves 4)

Ingredients:

280g penne
280g broccoli cut into florets
160g peas
25g butter

25g plain flour
300ml milk
1 tbsp wholegrain mustard
140g mature cheddar, grated

Directions:

1. Heat oven to 200°c/180°c (fan)
2. Cook the pasta, according to the packet instructions.
3. In a separate pan cook the broccoli & peas in boiling water for 5- 6 minutes.
4. Drain pasta & vegetables, leave to cool.
5. Heat the butter in a saucepan, stir in the flour for approx. 1 minute until a smooth paste forms
6. Then gradually add the milk, stirring well between each addition, bring to the boil, keep stirring, simmer for 2 mins
7. The sauce will begin to thicken, keep an eye on it so it doesn't catch or burn.
8. Remove from the heat, add 1 tbsp wholegrain mustard to the now thickened sauce & stir through.
9. Add half the cheese & seasoning to the sauce.
10. Tip the pasta, broccoli & peas into the sauce & spoon into an ovenproof dish.
11. Scatter over the remaining cheese & cook for 10 to 15 minutes until golden & bubbling.
12. Serve & Enjoy!

Chef: Ana Martin

How Did You Get Involved with YDWD?

I make sugar cookies weekly. I asked in the Mill Hill Facebook group if I could make doctors & nurses cookies for the hospitals & one of the coordinators said yes.

I make hospital themed cookies & my family help with the labelling & packing.

I am a scientist working in infectious diseases but also have a sister treating Covid Patients in a hospital in Madrid, so I wanted to help in any way I could.

Dish: Sugar Cookies (Ed. These are off the scale gorgeous)

Ingredients:

225g unsalted butter (2 sticks) cubed, cold
200g granulated sugar
1 tsp vanilla extract
1 tsp vanilla bean paste (optional)

65g corn-starch
¾ tsp kosher salt
2 eggs
400g all-purpose flour

Directions:

1. Preheat the oven to 190°c, & line baking sheets with parchment.
2. Cream the butter & sugar, just until smooth & combined.
3. Mix in the eggs until incorporated.
4. Add the flour, cornstarch, & salt, & mix on medium low speed.
5. The mixture will seem very dry & sandy at first, but after 3 to 5 minutes in the mixer it will gather itself into a ball & pull away cleanly from the sides of the bowl.
6. Stir in the vanilla. (If you do not have an electric stand & mixer with a paddle attachment, you may have to knead the dough by hand to fully bring it together.)
7. Roll the dough out between 2 sheets of parchment paper, to a thickness of ¼ inch.
8. Cut into shapes & bake for between 9 & 12 minutes (for appox. 2½ inch cookie).
9. Cool completely, then decorate with royal icing.

Chef: Benji Nathan

How Did You Get Involved with YDWD?

Since a young age I have always been in the kitchen, I then decided that I always wanted to be a chef. Because of that I decided to go to Westminster Kingsway College, where I am about to finish a Professional Chef Diploma. I was just 6 weeks away from my final practical exams when the pandemic started. So, I decided to put my trained profession into good use. Baking 150 portions of cake & bakes for the YDWD scheme each week.

Cooking is my passion & could not see myself doing anything else. It is what I love so all my passion & love is going straight to the heroes of the NHS.

Dish: 'Benji's Bakes Versatile Cookies'

Ingredients:

250g golden caster sugar
250g dark brown sugar
350g unsalted butter
2 tsp of vanilla
200g flavour *

3 eggs
530g plain flour
½ tsp of salt
½ tsp bicarbonate of soda

Directions:

1. Pre heat oven to 180°c
2. Cream the sugars & the butter until light & fluffy
3. Beat in the vanilla & slowly add the eggs one at a time
4. Fold in flour, bicarbonate of soda, salt, & your favourite flavour *
5. Roll into balls of your desired size (I suggest 30g) & refrigerate for 25 minutes, place on a baking tray leaving a large gap in-between
6. Bake for 7-10 minutes depending on the desired texture. 7 is chewy 10 has a snap.

Flavours:

* You can put almost anything into these cookies, I always add my flavour in 200g if it is a dry filling such as chocolate chips

- Triple chocolate - 65g white chocolate chunks, 65g milk chocolate chunks, 65g dark chocolate
- Peanut butter chocolate - 50g crunchy peanut butter or crushed honey roasted peanuts, 150 dark chocolate chips
- Raspberry & white chocolate - 50g freeze dried raspberries, 150g white chocolate chunks
- You can also add any chocolate bar on top. I love to snap of a piece of a snickers & place on top before baking.

Notes/Tips

- I love to keep balls or cooking dough in the freezer to bake fresh. Just pop a frozen ball of cookie dough into a pre heated oven & you have easy fresh cookies.
- This recipe can be used as a warm cookie dough. In an oven proof bowl place, a layer of cookie dough in the oven for 4 minutes. I like to add crumbled Biscoff biscuits & drizzled Nutella with some vanilla ice cream.

Chef: Beverley Szczech

How Did You Get Involved with YDWD?

I'm Beverley & am so pleased to be part of You Donate We Deliver. I responded to Linda Jacoby's Facebook Post on our Rock Choir Page asking of any of us could help by baking or cooking for the wonderful NHS staff. I sing with Linda & her daughter Rachel who is an NHS Doctor. I love cooking & am happy that I can play a small part in this fabulous setup. I'm baking a little extra each week & dropping to friends on my daily walk.

Dish: Veggie Chilli

Ingredients:

2 tins of mixed beans
2 chopped courgettes
2 tbsp of tomato puree
2 tbsp of bbq sauce
2 chopped carrots
Mexican spice
2 cartons of 550g chopped tomato with chilli & garlic
2 large chopped onions

Directions:

1. Sauté the chopped onions, carrot & courgettes in olive oil until soft
2. Add tomato puree & cartons of chopped tomato
3. Stir in the two tins of mixed beans
4. Add the BBQ sauce (1 tablespoon at a time to taste preference)
5. Add Mexican spice to taste
6. Serve with rice, quinoa, or tortilla wraps with sour cream, grated cheese & guacamole

Chef: Beverley Szczech

Dish: Tea Loaf

Ingredients:

285g raisins/sultanas
285ml of strong cold tea
1 large egg

200g soft brown sugar
280g self-raising flour

Directions:

1. Make the tea with approx. 5 tea bags for half a pint of tea
2. Pour the tea onto the raisins & brown sugar & leave to soak overnight
3. Mix the self-raising flour & egg into the raisins
4. Turn into lined tin & bake at 170°c for 1 hour 15 minutes. (use skewer to test if it is cooked through).

Top Tip - The top is likely to be done, but not cooked through, after an hour or so. If this is the case cover the top loosely with tin foil & let the heat cook it through

Chef: Beverley Szczech

Dish: Banana Muffins

Ingredients:

125g margarine
2 eggs
2/3 mashed bananas

175g sugar
220g self-raising flour

Directions:

1. Melt butter in pan, allow to cool
2. Mix the sugar in with the butter
3. Add the rest of the ingredients & mix well
4. Muffins: Pour into muffin cases & cook for 20 minutes at 170 °c

Top Tip – You can make this into a Banana Loaf by pouring the mixture into a lined loaf tin & cook for 45 minutes at 170 °c

Chef: Charlie D'Lima (Chef at Paul Ainsworth at No.6)

How Did You Get Involved with YDWD?

I have been professionally cooking for 2 years but working for Paul Ainsworth has shown me a team bond like no other, the entire group are working hard to feed NHS workers, homeless shelters, & vulnerable locals!

I contacted Sarah right from the beginning & her contagious enthusiasm had me go from making 40 meals a week to 500 a day. This was of course with the huge help from amazing volunteers like Dan Stern & the incredible facilities at Mill Hill School. It has been an honor to be a part of this blossoming charity from the very start! I hope some of my recipes will get people in the kitchen & cooking up an absolute storm!

The first recipe is widely used in Paul's restaurants & one of my favorite's! It is a great example of how you can get foraged food from the wild onto the plate in a few simple & safe steps. This recipe should get you a light fluffy focaccia every time & you can use whatever toppings you want.

Dish: Wild Garlic Focaccia Bread

Ingredients:

For the dough:
535g strong white flour
18g Maldon salt flakes
18g fresh yeast (or 9g dried yeast)
18ml olive oil
290ml luke-warm water

For the topping:
5g Maldon salt
50g wild garlic leaves
200ml olive oil

Directions:

For the Oil topping
1. To make the oil, lightly heat the oil to around 60° & blend it with the wild garlic/parsley leaves for 5 minutes.
2. Pass the oil through a j-cloth & set aside in the fridge

For the Dough
1. Mix the flour & salt in one bowl
2. Combine water, yeast, & olive oil separately
3. Slowly combine liquid to dry mix & knead for 10 minutes until window-pane effect is achieved.
4. Prove in lightly oiled bowl covered with cling film until doubled in size
5. Knock back & stretch into a large tin (about 30cmx20cm) so its approx. 2.5cm deep.
6. Allow to prove a second time, poking rosemary into the dough in a few places
7. Drizzle with your garlic/parsley oil & sprinkle generously with Maldon salt
8. Bake at 200 for 10 minutes & then reduce the temp to 180 & cook for another 10 minutes
9. After removing it from the oven feed it once more with the green oil so it stays nice & moist
10. Enjoy warm or hot

Chef: Charlie D'Lima

Dish: Vegetable Green Thai-Curry (Serves 4)

This delicious curry is great for using up leftover veg in the fridge & exciting the taste-buds. Its quick to knock up & goes great with rice or noodles. Its super healthy too so a great midweek meal.

Ingredients:

30ml sesame oil
1 tbsp coriander seeds
25g ginger julienned
3 kaffir lime leaves
1 butternut squash diced
1 red bell pepper diced
400ml coconut milk
1 bunch of fresh coriander

1 lemongrass stick sliced lengthways
1 green chilli chopped
2 cloves garlic sliced
1 Spanish/white onion diced
3 carrots diced
1 yellow bell pepper diced
zest of one lime

Directions:

1. Heat oil in a pan, add lemongrass, chilli, ginger, garlic, lime leaves & seeds to release aromas.
2. Add onion & sweat well, add all the vegetables, & cook through.
3. Add finely chopped coriander stalks (add Thai curry paste if using) & stir in
4. Add water to cover the vegetables & cook down, add coconut milk, & let reduce
5. Finish with fresh coriander & lime zest

Chef: Charlie D'Lima

Dish: Sticky Toffee Pudding with Salted Caramel Sauce (Makes 6 Portions)

The first time I met the 'You donate we deliver' team they had just had a big donation of fruits. I took a big bag of leftover dates & made one of the fluffiest sponges with them. It is so easy but delicious & will impress any dinner guests! You can pour it into individual molds to serve the desserts individually or make one big sponge cake to cut up into portions.

Ingredients:

For the Sponge:
125g pack dried, stoned dates
88g light muscovado sugar
¼ tsp bicarbonate of soda
½ tsp mixed spice

43g softened butter
1 medium egg, beaten
88g self-raising flour
¼ tsp vanilla extract

For the topping:
50g light muscovado sugar
75ml carton double cream

50g butter
½ tsp vanilla extract

Directions:

For the Sponge
1. Preheat the oven to 180°c, fan 160°c, gas 4. Lightly butter a 10 x 20cm traybake tin at least 2.5cm deep or 6 molds
2. Put the dates in a medium pan with 130ml boiling water. Bring to the boil then cook for 2-3 minutes to just soften the dates
3. Blitz on pulse till broken down or just mash with a fork
4. Put the butter & sugar in a mixing bowl & beat until light & creamy; gradually add the egg & beat well
5. Add the bicarbonate of soda to the dates – it will foam up – stir well
6. then add to the cake mixture with the flour, spice, & vanilla, & beat with a wooden spoon until combined
7. Pour the mixture into the tin & bake for 20-25 minutes or until the mixture feels firm to the touch in the center

For the Sauce
1. Meanwhile put all the sauce ingredients into a medium pan & bring to the boil. Cook for 8-10 minutes until thickened slightly.
2. Allow to cool then reheat when ready to serve. Drizzle a little over the top of the pudding & serve the remainder alongside it in a jug.

Chef: Crave Cakes – Sonal Vee & Alexandra Tawfik

How Did You Get Involved with YDWD?

Alex & I started Crave Cakes in June 2019. We met whilst doing our Masters together in 2002 & have been friends ever since. Our kids are now at school together & are very close friends.

We had both baked individually for our friends & families but in 2016 we made our first joint cake together for a friends 40th. We then spent 3 years making cakes together for everyone we know. Our cakes became more elaborate as our skills grew. If we weren't baking cakes, we were talking cakes. We had a lot of fun baking together & after lots of encouragement from our friend & families we took the plunge & started Crave Cakes.

At every celebration, cake is the one thing that makes everyone stop & go 'wow'. Crave Cakes is all about creating those 'wow' moments. We love the joy that our cakes bring to people. Also having someone tell us that our cakes are amazing is the ultimate

We know that other cake businesses had kept going during lockdown, but we felt that it would be unethical to call our business essential. So reluctantly we closed.

We were then introduced to 'You Donate… We Deliver' by our fiend Elena Hogg who was already cooking & donating. We jumped at the chance to be involved as we had been feeling very lost without being able to make our cakes to be enjoyed by others.

Even though Alex & I can't bake together as we did, we have loved being part of 'You Donate…We Deliver' & being able to send our cakes to hospitals has given us a sense of purpose during this time.

Below are three recipes that we hope you enjoy. If you want more recipes or tips, please follow @cravecakesuk on social media.

Chef: Crave Cakes – Sonal Vee & Alexandra Tawfik

Dish: Chocolate & Ginger Cake

Ingredients:

For the cake

200g butter (at least 70% fat) plus extra for greasing
4 tbsp full fat (or semi-skimmed) milk
175g self-raising flour
250g caster sugar
2 pcs stem ginger, finely chopped

50g cocoa powder
3 eggs
1 tsp baking powder
1 tsp ground ginger

For the filling & topping

225g icing sugar
2 tbsp stem ginger syrup
2 pcs stem ginger, finely shredded

115g butter (room temperature)
1 tbsp full fat (or semi-skimmed) milk

Directions:

1. Preheat the oven to 180°c (fan 160°c/350°f/Gas 4)
2. Grease the sandwich tins & the bottom of each with baking parchment
3. Put the cocoa powder into a large heatproof bowl & stir in 6 tbsp of boiling water, then add milk & mix to make a smooth paste
4. Add the remaining cake ingredients & combine using an electric h& whisk for 1-2 minutes. Do not over mix or the cake may not rise!!
5. Divide the cake mixture evenly between the prepared tins & level the tops
6. Bake for 25-30 minutes or until the cakes shrink away from the side of the tin & spring back when lightly pressed in the centre
7. Let the cakes cool for a few minutes before turning them out
8. Peel of the paper & turn the cakes the right way up & leave to cool on a wire rack
9. Make the filling & topping:
10. Sift the icing sugar into a large bowl
11. Add the butter, stem ginger syrup & milk & beat together using an electric hand whisk until well blended
12. Transfer one of the cakes to a serving plate & spread half the icing over the top
13. Place the second cake over the filling & cover the top with the remaining icing

Top Tip – Use the palette knife to draw large 'S' shapes to give a swirl effect, then decorate the edge with the shredded stem ginger

Chef: Crave Cakes – Sonal Vee & Alexandra Tawfik

Dish: Carrot Cake

Ingredients:

For the cake

300g soft light brown sugar
300ml sunflower oil
1 tsp bicarbonate of soda
1 tsp ground cinnamon
½ tsp salt
300g carrots, grated
50g shelled walnuts, chopped, plus extra, to decorate

3 eggs
300g plain flour
1 tsp baking powder
½ tsp ground ginger
¼ tsp vanilla extract
zest of half an orange
50g pecans, chopped, plus extra to decorate

For the icing

600g icing sugar (I only used 500g & it was fine)
250g cream cheese, cold (needs to be full fat - Philadelphia is best)

100g butter, at room temperature

Directions:

1. Preheat the oven to 170C. Prepare 3 x 20cm cake tins by greasing then lining the bottoms with greaseproof paper
2. Put the sugar, eggs & oil in a freestanding electric mixer with a paddle attachment
3. Beat until all the ingredients are well mixed (don't worry if it looks slightly split)
4. Slowly add the flour, bicarbonate of soda, baking powder, cinnamon, ginger, salt, orange zest & vanilla extract
5. Continue to beat until well mixed
6. Stir in the grated carrots & walnuts by h&. Pour into the prepared cake tins & smooth over
7. Bake in the preheated oven for 20–25 minutes (check your oven timings) or until golden brown & the sponge bounces back when touched
8. Leave the cakes to cool slightly in the tins before turning out onto a wire cooling rack to cool completely
9. To make the icing:
10. Beat the butter & sugar with the paddle attachment again until well mixed. Add the cream cheese, then beat again until well mixed
11. Turn the speed to high & continue to beat until light & fluffy but stop when you reach this point
12. If you over beat it the mixture will turn runny
13. When the cakes are cold, spread about one-quarter of the cream cheese icing over it with a palette knife (I used less)
14. Place a second cake on top & spread another quarter of the icing over it (again, I used less)
15. Top with the last cake & spread the remaining icing over the top & sides. Decorate with walnuts around the edges & chopped pecans on top

Chef: Crave Cakes – Sonal Vee & Alexandra Tawfik

Dish: Rose & Lemon Cupcakes

Ingredients:

For the cupcakes

175g room temperature butter
175g self-raising flour
zest of one lemon
1-2 tsp rose water

175g caster sugar
3 large eggs
juice of ½ lemon

For the buttercream

300g icing sugar
1-2 tsp rose water

150g room temperature butter
lemon juice to taste

Directions:

For the Cupcakes
1. Pre-heat oven to 160°c
2. Cream the butter & sugar until light & fluffy
3. Weigh out the flour & leave aside
4. Whisk the eggs in a jug & add to the butter & sugar mixture a little bit at a time
5. If you see your mixture curdling at all, add a teaspoon of the pre-weighed flour
6. Add the remaining flour & combine. Be careful not to over mix
7. Add the zest, lemon juice & rose water
8. Once everything is combined, fill the cupcakes cakes until roughly ⅔ full
9. Bake for 15-18 minutes. Check they are perfectly baked by inserting a skewer into the centre. It should come out clean

For the Buttercream
1. Beat the butter for a couple of minutes until it's softened
2. Add the icing sugar & beat until light & fluffy
3. Add in the rose water & lemon. Mix
4. Decorate using piping nozzles or spread over the cakes
5. Add sprinkles or fresh raspberries for some extra wow

Chef: Danine Irwin (CookCamp)

How Did You Get Involved with YDWD?

I am Danine Irwin. I am a home-cook & cookery teacher. I own CookCamp & I'm a qualified nutritionist & MasterChef quarter finalist!

I love, love, love food, cooking & cookbooks! A lot of the food I make is inspired by my Turkish/Spanish heritage, but I always love trying out any recipes.

During the 2020 Coronavirus lockdown all my work was temporarily suspended so I started off busying myself by making meals for the elderly & isolated; then I got involved with cooking for the NHS keyworkers & went on to make 100 meals each week, for wider distribution.

Who knows what will be around the next corner - but I do know that I will always love cooking & am more than happy to cook for anyone who may need.

Dish: 'Meatballs & Mash'

Ingredients:

For the meatballs

1kg beef mince
½ large bunch flat-leaf parsley
100g fresh breadcrumbs
A 'huge' squirt of ketchup

1 finely chopped onion
2 grated carrots
2 beaten eggs
salt & pepper

For the mash

600g potatoes
milk

butter
salt & pepper

Directions:

1. Mix all ingredients together really well, using your gloved hands
2. Roll the mince mixture into golf-ball-size meatballs
3. Gently soften & brown one or two sliced onions in a frying pan & then add the meatballs, browning them all over
4. Do this in batches so not to overfill the pan
5. Transfer the meatballs & the onions to an oven proof dish
6. Pour in a large carton of tomato passata or tomato pasta sauce
7. Cover with foil & oven cook for 30-45 minutes
8. In the meantime, make the mash potatoes with butter, milk & season salt & pepper to taste. (You can also serve with rice or spaghetti)
9. Serve up the cooked meatballs & the sauce atop a blob of creamy mash & a side of peas
   Other serving suggestions: With spaghetti & topped with parmesan or with rice & peas on the side

Buen provecho!

Chef: Debbie Morris

How Did You Get Involved with YDWD?

I was initially involved in the Elstree hub, making visors for the NHS & then also became part of Laura Bloomberg's Bushey hub & started making food. I have a love of cooking & always cook for friends & family, so during lockdown this meant I could channel my energies in a positive way. Being able to support the NHS & be a part of 'You Donate, We Deliver' has given me a great sense of purpose.

Dish: Carrot, Sweet Potato & Coriander Soup

Ingredients:

8 large carrots, peeled & sliced
1 large onion, chopped
4 tbsp of shopped coriander
100ml of double cream

2 sweet potato, peeled & cut in eighths
'Telma' chicken stock (vegetarian) x 2 tbsp (or to taste)
1 tsp of powdered cumin
1 tbsp of olive oil

Directions:

1. Get a large pot (holds around 3 litres) & Fry the Onion in oil until clarified, takes around 8 mins
2. Add the coriander, cumin & then vegetables & stir for a few minutes
3. Then add 2 litres of boiling water & the stock. Cover & simmer on medium heat for 20 mins & check veg is soft
4. When this is done, use a h& blender to liquidise the soup & make smooth
5. Check the seasoning & add more salt/pepper to taste, then add the cream & use the h& blender to quickly mix in
6. Should be a fairly thick consistency.
7. Great served with a fresh roll, as provided for the NHS

Chef: Debbie Morris

Dish: Roasted Vegetable Pasta Bake

Ingredients:

1 red pepper, deseeded & chopped
1 aubergine, sliced & chopped
fresh basil, 2 tablespoons roughly chopped
80g fresh spinach, chopped
1 tablespoon tomato puree
olive oil
grated mozzarella

1 yellow pepper, deseeded & chopped
1 medium onion, chopped
1 clove garlic, finely chopped
680g jar Passata
500g bag of fusilli
seasoning, salt & pepper

Directions:

1. Heat the oven on 180°c
2. Get a baking tray & lay out all the vegetables (except the spinach) & sprinkle over the garlic & fresh basil
3. Season liberally & pour over some olive oil, then mix, cover with foil & place in the oven for half an hour, remove foil for the last 5 mins
4. Bring large pot of water to the boil & cook the pasta for 8-10 mins, then drain
5. Mix the pasta in the large pot with all the roasted vegetables & add passata, tomato puree & chopped spinach. Mix well
6. Then place back in the baking tray & top with the Grated mozzarella. Bake for 30 mins on 170°c

Great served with salad!

Chef: Debbie Morris

Dish: Chicken Teriyaki Rice

Ingredients:

1 red pepper, deseeded & chopped
½ a pack of mushrooms, chopped small (so they are hidden from the kids view)
1 courgette, chopped small (so hidden from the kids view!!)
1 large carrot, chopped small (so hidden from the kids view!!)
2 chopped spring onions, for garnish
1 teaspoon fresh ginger, finely chopped
3 tablespoons of Teriyaki sauce
sesame oil
vegetable oil

1 yellow pepper, deseeded & chopped
1 small tin of sweet corn
1 medium onion, chopped
1 clove garlic, finely chopped
frozen petit pois
½ teaspoon of five spice
400g of chicken, sliced
2 eggs

Directions:

1. Marinate the chicken for an hour in the teriyaki sauce
2. Using a large wok, fry the onions until clear in vegetable oil, add garlic & ginger
3. Fry the chicken, add the five spice, & stir fry for10mins
4. Whisk the egg in a bowl, together with a little salt & the sesame oil
5. Push the onion & chicken to the edges of the wok with a spoon & then add a little more oil
6. Pour the egg mix into the middle of the wok & let it make a little omelette
7. Then chop it up with the wooden spoon & add the rest of the vegetables & stir fry for another 5 minutes
8. Add more teriyaki sauce if it gets too dry or a little water
9. Then add the rice in to the wok & stir fry it all together. Serve topped with spring onion

Top Tip – Other tasty additions would be chopped fresh coriander & some chilli oil!

Chef: Ellie Raefman

How Did You Get Involved with YDWD?

I have always been actively involved in various charities, so it just seemed natural to me to be able to help in any way I can during this time.

Earlier on this year I launched my new events & styling business, we were only up & running a few weeks before Covid-19 became a worldwide epidemic, sadly this meant all events were to be cancelled for the foreseeable future.

I spent the first couple of days in isolation feeling quite up & down, even though I knew eventually the world will right itself, it still didn't stop me from worrying about the unknown & feeling anxious. I decided that I didn't want to go through all of this feeling sad & worried & anxious the whole time, so I needed somewhere to focus my energies. I then had a conversation with my friend Sarah Laster, & she had mentioned she had spoken to her sister, a doctor, about the problems they were facing regarding food & supplies.

Although I no longer work as a chef, I did train at Leith's school of food & wine, & have worked as a chef over the years, so I decided that I would use the skills I have to be able to help others & also to have something good to focus on at this time. So, I got involved, my first cook I had neighbours in my street all banding together, helping me chop & peel vegetables from their homes, then dropping off at my door, pots & pans were lent to me, as I needed so much equipment on a bigger scale than I currently had.

The Greek Butter bean stew has been very popular (My Grandfather taught me this recipe & I know he would be looking down on me & be ever so proud of what I am doing)

Dish: Greek Butter Bean Stew (My Grandfather's Recipe) – Serves 4

Ingredients:

4 large carrots, medium sliced
2 Spanish onions, finely sliced
3 cans chopped tomatoes
4 fresh beef tomatoes (chopped)
1 tsp sugar
olive oil

1 pack celery, finely sliced
4 tins butter beans
2 tbsp tomato paste
4 cloves fresh garlic
1 small pack of flat leaf parsley, finely chopped
salt, pepper, paprika

Directions:

1. Heat the oil in a large saucepan & sweat the onions, carrots & celery until tender & the onions are soft & transparent, but not coloured
   Top Tip - put the heat on low, cover the vegetables in some GP paper & a lid
2. Add the minced garlic & turn up the heat for a few mins to cook out the garlic
3. Reduce the heat then add in the chopped & fresh tomatoes, sugar, puree, butter beans & simmer for 20-30 mins
4. The sauce should have started to thicken…
5. To finish adding some chopped fresh parsley & season to taste with the salt, pepper & paprika
6. Some crumbled feta & crusty bread are a lovey accompaniment

Chef: Ellie Raefman

Dish: Salmon Teriyaki with Egg Noodles & Stir Fry Vegetables (Serves 4)

Ingredients:

For the Teriyaki Marinade
100ml sesame oil
200ml vegetable oil
4 cloves of garlic, minced
300ml soy sauce

fresh ginger, 2in pieces, peeled & finely chopped
1 small bunch spring onions, finely chopped
2 tbsp honey
1 large pack coriander, chopped

For the rest of the dish
4 salmon fillets
1 large pack coriander, chopped
1 pack each of, baby corn, mangetout, bean sprouts
300ml sweet chilli sauce

400g egg noodles
100ml sesame oil
1 pack of tender stem broccoli

Directions:

1. Combine all the teriyaki sauce ingredients, add the salmon, & marinate for at least 2 hours or (ideally) overnight
2. Heat the oven to 190°c, add the salmon & ½ of the marinade to an oven proof dish & cook for 12-15 mins
3. Take the salmon out & cover with foil
   Top Tip – this allows the salmon to steam a little longer & stay moist
4. Meanwhile add the egg noodles to 1 litre of boiling water & half the sesame oil & bring to a simmer, cook for 5 mins until soft
5. Whilst the noodles are cooking heat the sesame oil in a in a wok or heavy bottomed frying pan
6. Add all the sliced vegetable & stir fry for 5 mins, until the vegetable are softened but still have some bite to them
7. For the last minute of cooking add the sweet chilli sauce & a handful of fresh coriander leaves
8. Heat up the remaining marinade
9. Drain the noodles & add to the vegetables
10. Serve the salmon on the bed of noodles & stir fry vegetable, pour over the remaining marinade

Top Tip – to get a fuller flavour, let the salmon marinade overnight

Chef: Ellie Raefman

Dish: Chicken Tikka Masala with Lentils & Spinach (Serves 4)

Ingredients:

100ml vegetable oil
4 tbsp tikka paste
500g chicken breast chunks (or 8 boned out thighs)
400g spinach leaves
1 pack coriander, chopped

1 Spanish onion, thinly sliced
1 can coconut milk
400g can green lentils, drained
200g natural yoghurt

Directions:

1. Heat half the oil in a large saucepan add the sliced onion & sweat down until soft, once cooked add in the tikka paste & combine
2. Meanwhile using the rest of the oil, brown the chicken for 5 minutes
3. Add the lentils, coconut milk & the cooked onions, cover & simmer for 15 minutes, stirring occasionally
4. Check the chicken is cooked through with no pink meat.
5. Then add the spinach leaves & allow to wilt down
6. To finish the dish off, once off the heat, stir in the natural yoghurt & chopped coriander to taste

Serving Tip - Serve with basmati rice, mango chutney & poppadum's

Top Tip - If you like your tikka to be slightly sweeter, add 3 tbsp of mango chutney whilst cooking

Chef: Emma Goldstein

How Did You Get Involved with YDWD?

I saw Sarah Laster's group on Facebook & reached out to see how I could help. I was put in touch with the Hampstead Garden Suburb hub coordinator & started to bake biscuits & cakes. I was told they needed more chefs & as I've been in events catering for 20 years, I thought I'd be able to help. I have done 200 meals & 150 cakes & biscuits. I've hung up my apron for now to be a rubbish home schoolteacher!!

Dish: Superfood Salad with Citrus Dressing – Serves 4

Ingredients:

For the Salad

250g purple sprouting broccoli
2 avocados
100g baby spinach
100g pomegranate seeds

150g soya beans
250g quinoa or couscous
A handful of parsley (coriander will also work)
100g pumpkin seeds, toasted in a dry pan

For the Dressing

zest & juice of 1 lemon (or lime zest)
zest & juice of 1 orange

2 tbsp Dijon mustard
2 tbsp rapeseed oil

Directions:

1. Cook the broccoli in a pan of boiling water for approx. 2 minutes
2. Add the soybeans & cook for further 1-2 minutes
3. Drain the vegetables & rinse in cold water to stop it cooking. Set aside
4. Add all the dressing ingredients & whisk with some seasoning
5. Peel & dice the avocado then add to the dressing (this will stop the avocado from going brown)
6. Add the quinoa, spinach, pomegranate, pumpkin seeds & cooked vegetables
7. Toss everything together & serve

Chef: Emma Goldstein

Dish: Vegetarian Couscous Salad

Ingredients:

For the Salad
250g couscous
2 courgettes, diced
1 red chilli, deseeded & finely chopped
1 x 400g can of chickpeas
2 tbsp olive oil

1 small cauliflower cut into small florets
1 large onion, diced
2 carrots, shredded or cut into small cubes
100g grated cheese
2 tbsp soy sauce

For the Dressing
olive oil

soy sauce

Directions:

1. Pre heat the oven to 190 °c (fan assisted)
2. Put the cauliflower & courgettes in a roasting tin & drizzle with olive oil
3. Scatter the cheese all over & roast in the oven for approximately half an hour. When cooked take out the oven & set aside
4. Peel & finely chop the onions & chilli & add to the cooled vegetables
5. Dice or shred the carrots & add to the vegetables
6. Cook the couscous according to the packet instructions
7. Now mix together all the vegetables together with the couscous & add the drained chickpeas
8. Add the dressing ingredients. Season with salt & pepper
9. Toss everything together & serve

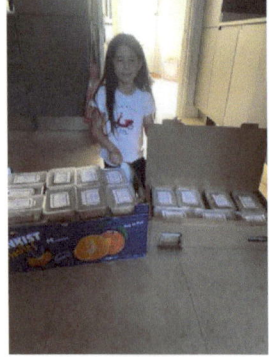

Chef: Gillian Jones (Gillian's Catering)

How Did You Get Involved with YDWD?

Gillian's Catering is a small catering company that specialises in world cuisine, we tend to work with clients & their budgets, so they get the best value for money & a menu that is made for them

This particular curry recipe was given to me from a friend who is Asian & is cooked in many Asian homes. When clients order this we always have so many compliments, as the mixture of heat & spice is good for all taste buds.

Dish: 'Gillian's Chicken Curry'

Ingredients:

500g chicken
4 cloves
1 stick / piece's cinnamon sticks
3 medium onions finely chopped
3 cloves of garlic, minced
salt approx. 1½ shallow tsp (or to taste)
3 heaped tsp coriander/cumin powder
pinch garam masala

4 tbsp vegetable / sunflower oil
4 cardamom pods
1 Star Anise
⅔ can of tin tomatoes, blitzed
1 square piece of ginger, minced
1 tsp Kashmiri chilli powder
1½ shallow tsp turmeric

Directions:

1. Heat a heavy base pan & add oil
2. Once hot, add cloves etc if using
3. Once whole spices have sizzled, add onions to the oil & brown gently, stirring occasionally ensuring not to burn them. Around 15-20 minutes
4. Once onions are nicely golden brown, add minced ginger & garlic, stirring all the time ensuring not to burn the garlic
5. Stir for a minute or two until you can smell the garlic aromas & then pour in the tomatoes
6. Now add the spices incl. salt. Stir & gently cook the sauce mixture for about 10 mins stirring occasionally
7. You will know when the sauce is ready as the oil will float to the surface
8. Finally add the chicken, stir thoroughly, turn down the heat, cover & cook for approx. 25 mins stirring occasionally
9. Remove from heat & add a pinch of garam masala & fresh coriander & stir through.

Enjoy!!

Chef: Helena Sharpstone

How Did You Get Involved with YDWD?

I live in North London with the wonderful & very long-suffering Alex, 3 lovely not so little ones - Guy, Zack & Ariella & 2 appallingly behaved cats called Jasper & Lola. I run a leadership & team development training & coaching business, volunteer at a local community café & am the Enfield Co-ordinator for The Hygiene Bank – a charity working to end hygiene poverty. I love to travel, entertain, & cook. As I can't do much of the first two, I'm concentrating on the last one!

I heard about YDWD from Sara Piler, the Totteridge Hub co-ordinator & I could not wait to get involved. I come from an NHS family. My darling Dad was a doctor & qualified when the NHS was in its infancy. He didn't retire until he was 80! Our eldest son Guy has just qualified as a doctor (my son the doctor) what timing! – & is about to enter the front line. I would love to think that one day, he might receive one of our meals. In the meantime, I am so happy to call myself one of the many YDWD cooks x.

Dish: 'Helena's Earl Grey Tea Bread' – Makes 15 Slices

Ingredients:

225g dried mixed fruit
440ml Earl Grey tea (made with 2 tea bags)
2 eggs
14g stevia

142g currants
1 level tbsp treacle or golden syrup
283g self-raising flour
1 tsp mixed spice

Directions:

1. Place the dried fruit in a large bowl & pour over the tea & treacle/syrup. Stir, cover, & leave overnight
   Top Tip - Leave the tea bags in until fairly strong
2. Lightly beat the eggs & stir into the mixture
3. Sift the flour & add to the mixture with the stevia & mixed spice. Stir to combine
4. Spoon into a lined 13 x 22 cm loaf tin & bake at 160°c/325°f/gas 3 for 1 hour or until a skewer comes out clean
5. Allow to cook & serve on its own or buttered. Yum!!

Chef: Helena Sharpstone

Dish: 'Helena's Chicken Casserole' (Serves 6)

I made this up one day when I was bored with the same old Friday night dinner. It's so tasty & not at all dry. It's a complete meal & you don't need to add anything. Maybe just some green vegetables if you're feeling pious! You can substitute the chicken breasts for legs & thighs if you prefer. I'm the only one in my family who likes white meat, so I do 3 legs/thighs per person instead.

20 minutes prep & 90 minutes cooking time.

Ingredients:

6 boneless chicken breasts
400g new potatoes quartered
600ml chicken stock
200g mushrooms, sliced
3 carrots, sliced
200g frozen peas
handful fresh parsley, chopped

2 tbsp oil
2 onions, diced
½ tin tomato puree
4 celery stalks, diced
1 red pepper, diced
1 yellow pepper, diced
salt & ground black pepper

Directions:

1. Heat the oil in a frying pan & fry the chicken pieces until brown on all sides. Place them in a large, ovenproof casserole dish
2. Fry the onions & add to the casserole
3. Fry the celery, peppers & mushrooms & add to the casserole
4. Add all the other ingredients to the casserole & season to taste
5. Cook in the oven for 1½ hours on Fan 180 °c / 350 °f / Gas 4
6. Serve as is or with a green vegetable. It's even better the next day!

Chef: Helena Sharpstone

Dish: 'Helena's Microwave Lentil Curry' (Serves 4 – generous portions!!)

This recipe is such a winner. It's a one pot, made in the microwave main dish, using no oil or butter, yet it never fails, tastes delish & I've yet to meet a child (or adult) who doesn't like it. & it's vegan!

5 minutes prep & 25 minutes cooking time.

Ingredients:

1 onion, finely chopped
250g red lentils
4 dessert spoons mango chutney

2 teaspoons hot or medium curry powder
750ml vegetable stock
salt & pepper to taste

Directions:

1. Place onion in a large bowl with water to half cover, cover with a lid & cook on HIGH for 2 minutes
2. Add curry powder, cover & cook for a further 1 minute
3. Stir in the remaining ingredients, cover & cook on HIGH for 20 minutes
4. Stir once or twice during this time & adding more water (but not too much) if necessary
5. Serve with boiled basmati rice & green peas or a mixed salad

Chef: Jeanne Wilson (Helena Sharpstones' Mum!!)

How Did You Get Involved with YDWD?

I'm 86 & I live in north west London with most of my 4 children & 9 grandchildren living nearby. One daughter & family live in the USA & I enjoy my annual visits across the pond to see them. I heard about YDWD from my daughter Helena who was already cooking for the Totteridge Hub & asked me if I would like to get involved too. I am really enjoying cooking for YDWD -what a fantastic initiative - & I hope all the recipients are enjoying some of my family favourites. It is keeping me busy in lockdown & I love doing something valuable with my time whilst I can't get out & about.

I spent 56 happy years married to my wonderful Victor, a GP & Dermatologist. He qualified as a doctor right at the start of the NHS & as a doctor's wife, I was very much part of his work & his practice. I have seen first-h& how our NHS workers devote themselves to caring for us & never more than now, under difficult & stressful circumstances. Victor was a massive fan of all things cake-related & whilst sadly, he is no longer with us, I think he would have wholeheartedly approved of the amazing deliveries of goodies (& meals!) to hospital staff. My second grandson Guy has just qualified as a doctor & is about to enter the NHS himself so there's a wonderful feeling of connection renewed. He has his late grandfather's stethoscope.

Dish: Cheese & Tomato Squares (Speedy Pizza!!)

Ingredients:

For the shortcrust pastry (Ed. yes make it yourself!!)

60g plain flour
60g margarine (or butter)
water to bind (1-2 tbs)

60g self-raising flour
2 tsp mixed dry herbs

For the topping

1 x tin chopped tomatoes
1 tbsp olive oil

1 onion, sliced very thinly
140g mature cheddar, grated

Directions:

1. Mix the herbs & flours in a bowl with the butter. Add the water & combine to make the pastry
2. Allow the pastry to rest for 15-20 minutes in the fridge
3. Meanwhile, fry the onions gently in the oil until soft
4. Add the can of tomatoes to the onions & simmer for about 15-20 minutes to allow most of the liquid to evaporate. Leave to cool
5. Roll the pastry on a dry surface & fit into a well-greased tin or baking paper approx. 10' x 8'
6. Spread the pastry with the cooled tomato & onion mixture & cover with a generous helping of cheddar cheese
7. Bake at 180°C (160°C fan) for approx. 45 minutes when the cheese should be melted & slightly brown, & pastry cooked
8. Cut into squares when cooled, eat warm or cold

Chef: Jeanne Wilson (Helena Sharpstones' Mum!!)

Dish: Spaghetti (or Pasta) al Pomodoro (Serves 6)

Ingredients:

550g spaghetti (or your favourite pasta)
1 clove garlic
1 tsp salt
small tsp sugar
parmesan or cheddar to grate on top

1-2 tbsp olive oil
2 x tins whole or chopped tomatoes
Few grinds black pepper
A couple of fresh basil leaves

Directions:

1. Heat the olive oil in a sauté pan (with a lid) or deep-frying pan
2. Allow the garlic cloves to flavour the oil for a few seconds
    Top Tip – if you want a stronger garlic flavour, in which case leave in the pan until the sauce is finished
3. Pour the content of the 2 tins of tomatoes in a food processor & pulse for a few seconds to make smooth, then pour into the pan
4. Add the salt, pepper & sugar (to taste), bring to the boil, cover with the lid & reduce heat to simmer gently for 20 minutes
5. For the final 5-6 minutes add the basil leaves, remove these when the sauce is finished
6. In the meantime, bring a large saucepan of water to the boil & add salt. Add the spaghetti & cook according to the packet instructions
7. Drain the spaghetti, keeping some of the starchy cooking water
8. Then add the spaghetti & a ladle of cooking water to the sauce, stirring in to coat all of the spaghetti
9. Serve & sprinkle with grated parmesan or cheddar

Chef: John Partridge (Actor)

How Did You Get Involved with YDWD?

I got involved with 'You Donate…We Deliver' through my good friend Scott Maslen. Having recently released my own cookbook, I wanted to do something to help our NHS Heroes. 100 portions of my Thai Green Curry later…

Dish: 'The Jon's Thai Green Chicken Curry'

Ingredients:

For the Thai green curry paste

100g shallots, roughly chopped
15g fresh root ginger, peeled and roughly chopped
2 medium-hot green chillies, roughly chopped
10 black peppercorns
1 tsp shrimp paste
2 tbsp Sugar

50g garlic cloves, roughly chopped
5 lemon grass stalks, roughly chopped
3 lime leaves, roughly torn
15g galangal paste
2 tbsp coconut oil or vegetable oil
juice of a lime

For the rest of the dish

1 whole chicken
1 to 2 tins coconut milk (400/800 ml)
1 lemongrass stalk bruised
3 tbsp vegetable oil

500 ml chicken stock
1 knob of ginger
500 g basmati rice

Directions:

1. Place a whole chicken into a heavy based pan. Pour in the chicken stock & then top up with cold water to cover the chicken completely
2. Add a knob of ginger & one lemongrass stalk. The pan will be very full. Don't panic it won't boil over!
3. Bring the pan to the boil then turn down the heat to a low simmer cover with the lid & poach the chicken for 1 hour 30 mins
4. Soak the rice in water for at least 30 mins
5. Put all the paste ingredients except the sugar & oil in the food processor & blitz
6. Heat the oil in a heavy based pan then add the paste & gently fry over a medium heat for 3 minutes
7. Then add the coconut milk, simmer for 3 minutes, then add the sugar
8. Now the chicken is cooked remove it from the broth saving 2 cups (around 500ml of the stock)
9. Remove all the meat from the bird, shred it & add it to the coconut milk. Next add the sugar & the juice of a lime or two. Season to taste
10. In a large saucepan heat vegetable oil & then add the soaked rice coating all the grains in the oil
11. Next add the 2 cups or 500 ml of saved broth & 500 ml of water.

Top Tip – When cooking rice, you want double wet to dry… so 500g rice cooks in 1000 ml fluid!

12. Bring it to the boil, then cover with the lid and turn down to a low heat and simmer for ten minutes
13. Then leave the lid on but turn the heat off for another ten minutes
14. Remove the lid and using a fork give it a good fluff! This will give your perfect fluffy rice every time

Serve….

Chef: Lindsey Jacobs (Creative Cuisine)

How Did You Get Involved with YDWD?

My name is Lindsey Jacobs, my business is Creative Cuisine, & we cater for all your functions, from a delicious Friday night dinner, delivered to your door, with all the trimmings to a full function up to 250 guests.

I was approached by Vicky Baruch who initially asked if I would be prepared to make some soup for the NHS & before I knew it I was cooking up to 100 meals a day. Whilst my business has taken a downturn due to the Virus I decided that I would put my skills to good use & help the **You Donate we Deliver** organisation, at least I feel like I am doing my bit for the cause & look forward to cooking for my clients soon.

Dish: Rich Spaghetti Bolognaise – Serves 4 – Cooking time 25min

Ingredients:

2 tbsp olive oil
1 large carrot, finely chopped
500g steak mince
1 tbsp dried oregano
1 whole bay leaf
800g chopped tomatoes
100ml red wine
1 pinch salt & pepper

1 large onion, finely chopped
1 celery stalk, finely chopped
3 cloves garlic, crushed
1 tsp basil, dried
1 tbsp tomato puree
2 x 400g tins tomato passata
1 whole beef stock cube
400g spaghetti

Directions:

1. Heat the oil in a large pan over a medium-low heat
2. Cook the onion, carrot & celery for 12-15 minutes until softened
3. Increase the heat & add the beef mince. Cook until browned all over, breaking it up into small pieces with a wooden spoon
4. Add the garlic, oregano, basil & bay leaf & cook for another 5 minutes
5. Stir in the tomato purée, chopped tomatoes, passata, red wine & beef stock cube
6. Season generously & cover with a lid. Simmer for one hour, stirring occasionally, until thick
7. Bring a pot of salted water to the boil & cook the spaghetti according to the package instructions. Drain a stir into the Bolognese sauce.

Top Tip – Always add the pasta/spaghetti to the sauce!!

Chef: Lindsey Jacobs

Dish: Moroccan Vegetable Tagine

You can use almost any kind of vegetables in this stew; its perfect for emptying the fridge.

Ingredients:

3 tbsp olive oil
3 cloves garlic, minced
1-2 tbsp grounded cinnamon
10 dried apricots
2 cups canned chopped tomatoes
a handful fresh coriander
1 zucchini, cut into 2-inch pieces
pinch of salt
a handful raisins

1 large onion, roughly chopped
1 inch fresh ginger, minced (or 1 tsp grounded)
1 tsp cumin
2-3 tsp harissa paste (or dried harissa)
1 lemon, juice & zest
1 small pumpkin, peeled & cut into 2-inch pieces
1 sweet potato, peeled & cut into 2-inch pieces
3 carrots, peeled & cut into 2-inch pieces
½ cup chickpeas/garbanzo beans, pre boiled

Directions:

1. In a clay pot: Heat olive oil in a large clay pot & sauté the onion for a few minutes until it softens
2. Add garlic, ginger & the spices & stir around before adding harissa, tomatoes, lemon juice & fresh cilantro
3. Bring the tomato sauce to a boil & then lower the heat
4. Add pumpkin, carrots, sweet potato, zucchini & apricots
5. Stir around, make sure that all vegetables are somewhat covered in tomato sauce
6. Put the lid on & simmer for about an hour. Stir carefully once or twice, otherwise leave the lid on
7. In a tagine: Prepare the tomato sauce according to the instructions above. Transfer it to the tagine
8. Add the vegetables, attach the lid & put in the oven on low temperature for at least an hour
9. When the vegetables feel tender, add chickpeas & raisins & let everything simmer for 5 minutes before removing it from the oven
10. Serve the tagine in bowls together with cooked quinoa or couscous. Sprinkle with almonds, lemon zest & fresh spices

Chef: Madeline Berg

How Did You Get Involved with YDWD?

My name is Madeline Berg & I have been cooking for 'You Donate…We deliver' for about 5 weeks.

I cook once or twice a week & make 100 vegetarian meals including cauliflower, potato & chickpea curry, lentil, vegetable & tomato pasta, cheese & pasta with vegetables & vegetarian chilli with cheese. I choose recipes that are nutritious, filing & hopefully tasty. Many are vegan friendly too.

I am a secondary school teacher who works in a mainstream secondary school with pupils with special needs. This is only part time, so I have some time to cook.

I was introduced to this project through my friend who is a chef Lindsey Jacobs & although it's hard work I enjoy giving something back at these times.

Dish: Vegetarian Curry

Ingredients:

For the flavour base
1 splash olive oil
1 heads garlic cloves, chopped
2 tbsp chili powder
2 tbsp dried oregano
1 onion, chopped
2 carrots, small cubes
2 tbsp cumin

For the chilli
1 x 800g can chopped tomatoes
250 ml water
1 400g can kidney beans, drained & rinsed
1 tsp salt
fresh coriander sprigs
1 x 150g can tomato paste
200g pearl barley
1 chipotle pepper in adobo sauce or one chilli pepper, minced
1 x 400g canned or frozen sweetcorn
grated cheese

Directions:

1. Heat oil in large pan. Add onions, minced garlic & carrots. Cook until slightly softened – about 5 minutes
2. Add the dried herbs & spices & cook for another 1-2 minutes until aromas released
3. Add the tomatoes, tomato paste, water & pearl barley. Cook for 1 minute
4. Add beans, chilli pepper & salt, stir & bring to the boil. Reduce heat, cover & simmer 25 minutes until barley is tender. Stir occasionally
5. Add sweetcorn & cook for a further 1-2 minutes
6. Serve topped with grated cheese & sprig of coriander

Chef: Martine Glass

How Did You Get Involved with YDWD?

I heard about 'You Donate…We Deliver' from a friend of mine & wanted to help especially as my dad was in hospital battling with COVID 19. I was added to Sara Piler's group. It helps to know that we are doing something to help the amazing NHS staff.

As for me, I'm married with 3 grown children & a lovely granddaughter. I have a voluntary job helping to run a community cafe, I paint & make objects from glass & recently started experimenting with 3D optical illusion art. So, plenty to keep my busy during lockdown

Dish: 'Grandma's Salmon Balls' (Delicious!!)

Ingredients:

large tin of salmon	2 eggs
matzo meal or similar	plain flour
salt & pepper	vegetable oil

Directions:

1. Empty tin of salmon with liquid into a bowl, I remove the skin but you don't need to
2. Add 1 egg, seasoning & a tablespoon of matzo meal
3. Really mash until you have a smooth mixture
4. With wet hands roll into small balls, dip in seasoned flour, followed by a beaten egg & finally seasoned matzo meal
5. Roll again & pop in fridge for a while or overnight Fry in hot oil
6. Try one first as you may need to add more seasoning. & drain on paper

Top Tip - These freeze well (I had to make extra as my children love them)

Chef: Martine Glass

Dish: Date 'Crumble' Squares (Makes 16-20 Crumble Squares)

These squares have a chewy oatmeal crust with a crisp, crumbly topping & a smooth date filling

Ingredients:

1¾ cups rolled oats
2½ cups stoned dates
½ tsp baking powder
1 cup butter

1 cup plain flour
1 cup sugar, brown if possible but white is fine
½ cup baking soda
2 tsp lemon juice

Directions:

1. Pre-heat your oven to 180°C (170°C fan)
2. Line an 8" or similar size tin
3. Cut up the dates, add the baking soda, 1 cup of boiling water & the lemon juice
4. Stir & pop into the microwave for a minute, leave to get soft, you may need to heat again if the dates are hard
5. When soft blitz with a stick blender
6. Combine oats, flour, sugar, & baking powder plus a touch of salt if using unsalted butter
7. Crumble quickly with fingers although I use a knife to start with, until you have a 'crumble mix'
8. Press half the mix into the tray, pressing hard, cover with mashed dates & them cover the rest of the mix, pressing down lightly
9. Cook for around 50 minutes until crispy & golden. Cool down & pop in the fridge before cutting. Freezes well

Top Tip – You can use a mixture of dates & cranberries

Chef: Natasha Gibbens (Forever Vegan Kitchen)

How Did You Get Involved with YDWD?

My name is Natasha & my company is Forever Vegan Kitchen. I became vegan nearly 2 years ago after toying with the ideas of having a few plant-based meals a week but then spoke to a vegan friend & did my own research & then went vegan overnight! My son took part in Veganuary & whilst cooking up batches of meals for him, Forever Vegan Kitchen was born.

A plant-based meal service for those who don't know where to start!

I am based in Barnet & offer a wide range of vegan meals, delivered to your door. I am on Deliveroo & Indie Hob (a new online platform for independent chefs) & I also cater for events & trade at food festivals. My meals are delicious, varied, & good for your health & the planet!

I became involved in the project when I was contacted by a friend who had been cooking from the start & asked if I would come on board & of course I said yes immediately. Such an amazing project, serving up nutritious meals to the angels on the frontline, which I am immensely proud to be part of.

Dish: The Best Vegan Banana Bread Ever!!

Ingredients:

200g plain flour
60g dairy free butter
½ tsp bicarbonate of soda
115g dark chocolate chips
Pinch of salt

115g light soft brown sugar
3 medium size ripe bananas
1 tsp baking powder
Approx. 100ml dairy free milk (almond, soya, oat etc)

Directions:

1. Mash the bananas in a large bowl & set aside
2. In another large bowl combine the sifted flour, butter, sugar, salt, baking powder & bicarbonate of soda
3. Rub the mixture together to make very fine crumbs
4. Add the bananas & milk & mix until incorporated. You may need to add more milk, the mixture should be like a thick custard
5. Line a loaf tin & cook for approx. 40 minutes at 160 degrees. Keep checking the cake with a skewer
6. Once baked, remove from oven & leave the cake for a few minutes in the tin, then transfer to a cooking rack

Top Tip - You can also add chopped nuts to the mixture prior to baking (allergen)

Chef: Natasha Gibbens

Dish: 'Banging Vegan Chilli & Couscous' (Ed: & it is Banging!!)

Ingredients:

For the Chilli

400g chestnut mushrooms
2 tbsp olive oil
1 red pepper
2 tbsp tomato purée
2 x 400g tinned tomatoes
1 x 400 kidney beans
2 tbsp maple syrup
2 tbsp chilli powder
1 tsp smoked paprika
1 tsp oregano
salt & pepper

1 brown onion
4 garlic cloves
1 green pepper
2 tbsp balsamic vinegar
1 x 400g black beans
100g green lentils
10g dark chocolate
1 tsp cumin
½ tsp ground cinnamon
30 g fresh coriander

For the Couscous

200g couscous
200ml veg stock
1 tbsp olive oil

50ml lemon juice
knob of dairy free butter
salt & pepper

Directions:

1. Rinse the lentils in a sieve with cold water, then boil for 15 minutes, drain, rinse under cold water & set aside
2. Dice the onion & mince the mushrooms in a food processor or chop them very finely
3. Put the oil in a heavy based saucepan, then add minced mushrooms. Cook for 5 minutes & then set aside in a bowl
4. Add diced onions to pan & then chop coriander, including stalks & add the stalks with the minced garlic to the pan, save the leaves for later
5. Cook for a few minutes
6. Then add diced peppers, cook for a further 5 minutes
7. Next add all of the spices & oregano & stir regularly
8. Then add tomatoes, maple syrup, balsamic vinegar & season with salt & pepper
9. Put the heat on a moderate temperature to let the sauce reduce
10. Then add the tins of beans, cooked lentils & dark chocolate & simmer for 10 minutes with the lid off
11. Add water if you need to achieve the right consistency. Stir frequently to prevent it from catching on the bottom of the pan
12. Whilst this is cooking prepare the couscous.
13. Put stock, butter, oil & salt into a pan, bring to the boil & add couscous
14. Cook for 5 minutes then take off heat & leave in pan with lid on to steam
15. Fluff up with a fork & then add black pepper to taste & lemon juice. Stir well
16. Stir the coriander leaves into the sauce & serve in bowls with the couscous.

Chef: Natasha Gibbens

Dish: Thai Red Curry

Ingredients:

For the Thai Red Paste

1 tsp cumin seeds
2cm piece fresh ginger
4 garlic cloves
3 fresh red chillies
½ roasted red pepper from a jar
3 kaffir lime leaves
10g coriander (plus extra for garnish)
50ml water

2 tbsp coriander seeds
5 shallots
2 lemon grass stalks
1 tsp black peppercorns
2 tbsp tomato purée
½ lime
2 tsp salt

For the Curry Sauce

1 red pepper
1 green pepper
160g cherry tomatoes or baby plums
50g mangetout
1 x 400g tin coconut milk
1 tbsp coconut sugar (or regular sugar)
4 tbsp soy sauce or tamari (gluten free)

1 fresh red chilli
200g mushrooms
60g fine green beans
2 tbsp vegetable oil
150ml veg stock
2 tbsp agave nectar

Directions:

1. Make the paste - Put the cumin & coriander seeds in a small frying pan & dry fry them to release their aromas. Add these to a blender
2. Peel & roughly chop the ginger, garlic & shallots, Deseed & chop up the chillies & add all these to the blender with the lemon grass
3. Add the roasted pepper, lime leaves, peppercorns, coriander, tomato purée, lime juice, salt & half of the water
Top Tip – you can add more as necessary - enough to loosen the paste
4. Blend until smooth
5. Cut up & deseed the peppers & chop the mushrooms & green beans in half
6. Put the oil into a wok & get it hot
7. Add 100g of the paste (save the rest for another day) & cook for a few minutes until it has deepened in colour & smells amazing
8. Then add the coconut milk, stock, sugar, agave, soy sauce, all the vegetables & sliced red chilli
9. Leave to simmer for 10 minutes, stirring occasionally
10. Serve with white rice & garnish with coriander leaves

Chef: Penny Beral (Catering by Penny Beral)

How Did You Get Involved with YDWD?

I have run my catering business Catering by Penny Beral for 36 years, mainly catering family parties & life cycle events. When I was approached by Jackie Commissar to cook, I was delighted as literally my work had dried up overnight. Being able to contribute in a small way to help feed NHS staff has been amazing & I have thoroughly enjoyed being part of the cooking team. I have always loved being creative with a few ingredients & producing lots of meals.

My only helper is my husband video producer, commis, his main task is to lid, label & load. I could not have done this without his support.

Dish: Risotto 'NHS'

Ingredients:

2 cups basmati rice
1 tin tomatoes
2 carrots
2 garlic cloves
Seasoning
Olive oil

500g beef mince
2 tbsp tomato puree
1 large onion
1 red pepper
2 vegetable stock cubes

Directions:

1. Finely chop or put in food processor onions, carrots & garlic
2. Add red pepper. Place this in a frying pan with the olive oil, cook gently until beginning to get soft, add the mince & stir well to break it up
3. Cook for about 10 minutes, add the tomatoes, tomato puree, seasoning, 1 stock cube & gently simmer for half an hour
4. Take the rice & rinse in a sieve until the rice runs clear, removing the starch. Place in a saucepan with 4 cups of water
5. Bring to the boil, once boiled reduce heat, stir once & place a lid on pan
6. Cook until all the water has evaporated. Turn off & leave with lid on
7. Once the mince is cooked through & the rice finished. Add the rice to the mince mixture, bring to the boil & allow the liquid to reduce
8. Serve with chopped parsley

Chef: Penny Beral

Dish: 'NHS Vegetable Curry' – Serves 4

How to make curry out of a few ingredients, feeding 100!! This recipe is based on feeding 4!!!

Ingredients:

1 large baking potato	1 large onion
2 carrots	1 aubergine
½ cauliflower	1 pepper
1 tin tomatoes	2 tbsp tomato puree
Any tins of beans or chickpeas	curry powder
2 tbsp stock powder or 2 stock cubes	Fresh ginger
2 garlic cloves	Sunflower oil
2 heaped tbsp mango chutney	Basmati rice

Directions:

1. Slice the onions, & crush garlic cloves
2. Heat the oil in a frying pan add the sliced onions & garlic.
3. Heat through as the onions begin to cook add the curry powder & gently allow the spices to cook through
4. Cube the potato & bring to the boil, drain the water, & reserve
5. Chop the remaining vegetables, place in a baking tin
6. Add the tomatoes, beans & tomato puree, mix together, add the potatoes & the cooked onions. Stir well
7. Use the potato liquid & add to the stock, mix well & add to the vegetables. Cover with foil & cook in a low oven 160°C or gas 4 for an hour
8. The vegetables should all be soft & well mixed together
9. Cook the rice according to the packet
10. Serve curry on a bed of rice & mango chutney

Chef: Penny Beral

Dish: 'Store Cupboard Banana Cake' (or Muffins or Both!!!)

I have sorted out my store cupboard. I took everything out of each shelf & gave it all a good clean. I found some flaked almonds, a mix of pumpkin seeds & cranberries, brown sugar, flour. Immediately I thought I could make a Banana Cake. (Ed. The mind of a chef, not a banana mentioned in how it came about, but Penny thought, Banana Cake!!!)

Ingredients:

250g self-raising flour (could be gluten free)
175g brown sugar
Flaked almonds, cranberries & pumpkin seeds
1 tsp cinnamon

250g pure spread
4 eggs
2 bananas (getting a bit brown!)

Other additions:
chocolate drops, cherries, raisins, dried apricots, dates

Directions:

1. Put all the ingredients into a mixing bowl, using a h& whisk or a machine beat everything together
2. If it looks a bit thick add some milk or boiling water
3. Line a 2lb loaf tin with baking parchment or well grease the tin. You can also make muffins, use a muffin tin lined with paper cases
4. Once cooked leave to cool & then serve with a cuppa
5. These cakes will freeze. I made 1 loaf tin & 10 muffins with this mixture
6. Bake the cake for 40 minutes on 165°C, Gas Mark 4. Muffins take about 15 minutes.

Top Tips - This recipe has less sugar than you might expect, because of the natural sweetness of the dried fruits & bananas
If you haven't got self-raising flour you can use plain or wholemeal flour & add 1 tsp baking powder
For a vegan alternative replace the eggs with 1½ tsp cider or white wine vinegar

Chef: Phillipa Bellman (Phillipa Bellman Catering)

How Did You Get Involved with YDWD?

I normally have a small catering company called Phillipa Bellman Catering, due to covid 19 I found myself doing very little cooking for clients & so I heard about YDWD through a friend. I have been cooking meals every week for our lovely, & hard-working NHS staff. It has been my pleasure, & this is one of my favourite recipes.

Dish: Chicken Tikka Masala NHS

Ingredients:

8 skinned & boned chicken thighs*
1 medium red onion
Vegetable oil
1 red chilli
3 large cloves garlic
1 tsp curry powder red
2 tsp garam masala powder
Salt & pepper to taste

500g of yogurt (fat free or full fat)
1 bunch of coriander
1 lemon
1 inch fresh ginger
3 tsp tomato puree
2 tsp ground cumin
1 small tub of double cream (or you can use yogurt)

*You can use chicken breast cut into large cubes

Directions:

1. Roughly chop garlic, half the onion, ginger, 1 chilli & coriander put in a small food processor
2. Add 1 tsp garam masala & 1 tsp cumin & 2 tbsp yogurt & Blend mix in half of the yogurt & stir
3. Cut chicken thighs into large cubes or leave whole
4. Put in a bowl squeeze half the lemon juice & sprinkle the red chili powder with a pinch of salt & mix well, leave for half an hour
5. Pour over the marinade, mix well & marinate for 3 hours or overnight in the fridge
6. Put the chicken onto a baking tray & put under a hot grill for approx. 10 mins each side, the chicken should have little black corners
7. In a deep-frying pan add a little oil & the other half of the onion chopped – cook till softened
8. Add 1 tsp of Cumin & Garam Masala – stir well for 1 minute – add 3 tsp tomato puree & cook for another minute
9. Add the cream or yogurt & stir for another minute
10. Add the chicken & all the juices to the pan & stir gently
11. Add a small bunch of chopped coriander, keeping a little back for garnish – add a pinch of salt & pepper if required
12. Simmer for 10-12 minutes checking the chicken is cooked through
13. Serve with basmati rice, sprinkle chopped coriander over the top & chutneys of your choice

Top Tips – If you have yogurt over, add 2 tsp of mint sauce, pinch of salt & pepper & mix well for a Mint Yogurt sauce
The chicken after marinating can also be put on skewers for the BBQ or put on a griddle with no sauce as Chicken Tikka

Chef: Renee Yarshon (Wilson Vale Catering Management)

How Did You Get Involved with YDWD?

I am a chef & have been for over 30 years, cooking comes from my soul, it's my greatest passion. I gained my stripes at the best Catering School Westminster College in London & then worked my way up through the ranks in various establishments with some of the most incredible chefs gaining great skills & knowledge.

Covid-19 has given me the time to be able to reflect on what I do & share my passion with others.

When Lockdown began, I wanted to help, I cooked & took food to my local chemist & The East of England Paramedics but didn't have the resource to do anymore. I knew there must be something more & through a wonderful collaboration of Music & Donation through the amazing Paulie V Rewind to M & H I met Natalee Powell from YDWD & am now part of this amazing group helping to feed our incredible NHS staff.

Dish: Pesto Roasted Chicken with Roast Potatoes & Vegetables

Ingredients:

For the Pesto
1 bunch of basil
1 clove garlic
50g pine nuts (optional)
50g grated parmesan
150ml olive oil

For the Roasted Chicken
8 chicken thighs
3 red onions
1 aubergine
500g new potatoes
3 courgettes
3 peppers
1 punnet cherry tomatoes
Handful of basil leaves

Directions:

1. Make the pesto. Place the basil & garlic into a food processor & blitz together
2. Add the cheese, & pine nuts (if you are using them) & blitz for another 30-40 seconds. Add the oil & whizz together. Season to taste
3. Coat the chicken in half the pesto & leave to marinate for at least 1 hour. (this can be done the day before)
4. Once the chicken has marinated for at least an hour, place it on a tray & roast for approximately 40 minutes
5. Cut the potatoes in half, length ways toss in oil, salt & pepper, & place on a tray & roast for about 30-40 minutes until golden & tender
6. Wash all the vegetables. Cut the courgettes, onions, peppers & aubergine into a chunky dice & toss with oil, & season
7. Place onto trays to roast in the oven for about 20 minutes until golden & tender
8. Cut the tomatoes into halves & lay on a tray sprinkle with oil & salt & pepper & roast for about 10 minutes
9. Tip the roasted vegetables into a bowl & stir in the tomatoes
10. Put the potatoes in a bowl tear the basil leaves & sprinkle on the top
11. Place the chicken on a serving plate & drizzle with the remaining pesto & serve

Chef: Renee Yarshon

Dish: Lamb Kofte with Yoghurt Flatbread & Tzatziki

Ingredients:

For the Lamb Kofte

200g minced lamb
1 clove of garlic crushed
2 tsp of toasted crushed coriander seeds
Handful of chopped coriander
Juice of 1 lemon
50g breadcrumbs

1 finely chopped onion
2 tsp of toasted crushed cumin seeds
1 chopped chilli
Handful of chopped mint
1 tbsp Greek yogurt

For the Yoghurt Flat Bread

200g Greek yogurt
Juice of 1 lemon
Handful chopped coriander

200g self-raising flour mixed with 1 tsp baking powder
½ tsp crushed garlic

For the Tzatziki

200g Greek yogurt
tsp crushed garlic
Squeeze of lemon juice

½ Cucumber deseeded & grated
Handful chopped dill
Salt & Pepper

Directions:

1. Prepare the flat bread dough by mixing the yogurt with the lemon juice, coriander, garlic & salt & pepper
2. Add half the flour mix & stir together, add the rest of the flour & mix to form a soft dough
3. Using your h& mould, the dough together until you can form it into a ball. Place back in the bowl & cover with cling film
4. While the dough is resting make the Kofta mix. Place all the ingredients into a bowl & season with salt & pepper
5. Mix well to ensure the meat is combined with all the spices, herbs, lemon, & yogurt
6. Shape the koftas by taking a small handful & rolling into a ball, then roll into a tube shape & pinch each end
7. Repeat this with the remaining meat
8. Line a baking tray with foil & place a cooling rack on top lay the Koftas on the rack ready to grill
9. Grill for 10-15 minutes turning the koftas until they are golden on both sides & fully cooked in the middle. Keep warm

   Top Tip – As an Alternative Koftas can be cooked on a BBQ or baked in the oven

10. Remove the cling film from the bowl with the flat bread dough & place the dough onto a floured surface
11. Cut the dough into 6 pieces. Flour your hands & gently mould each piece into a ball
12. Using a rolling pin roll out each ball into a circle. Each time you roll make sure you lift & turn the dough, so it does not stick
13. Heat a frying pan or griddle & place the flat breads in one at a time
14. Cook for 1-2 minutes until the bread starts to turn golden brown underneath & bubbles start rising turn the flat bread over & repeat
15. Remove from the pan & place the breads on tray sprinkle lightly with garlic oil
16. To make the Tzatziki place the grated cucumber, garlic, lemon juice, salt & pepper in a bowl & mix in the yogurt
17. Place a flat bread on a plate, with the Koftas top with a good spoonful of Tzatziki & Serve

Chef: Renee Yarshon

Dish: Moroccan Spiced Chicken with Almond Couscous & Roasted Butternut Squash – Serves 4

A delicious take on Tagine style cooking the almond couscous & butternut add delicious sides to make this a great complete meal.

Ingredients:

For the Marinade
1-2 teaspoons of Harissa Paste

A little olive oil

For the Chicken
4 chicken breasts cut into cubes or 8 chicken thighs
500ml chicken stock
2 tsp grated ginger
2 tsp ground cinnamon
2 tsp smoked paprika
50g chopped dates
1 tin chickpeas
Handful chopped coriander

1 large onion sliced
2 cloves of garlic crushed
2 tsp ground cumin
2 tsp ground Turmeric
100g chopped dried apricots
1 tin chopped tomatoes
1 lemon cut into wedges
Handful chopped flat parsley

For the Couscous
300g couscous
1 chilli finely sliced
100g ground almonds
Handful chopped mint
Handful chopped flat parsley

Lemon juice
4 spring onions sliced at an angle
1 red onion finely diced
Handful chopped Coriander
Handful Toasted flaked almonds

For the Roasted Butternut squash
1-2 butternuts peeled cut in half & deseeded
1 tsp chilli flakes
Greek yogurt

1 tsp cumin
Olive oil
Honey & pomegranate seeds to garnish

Directions:

1. Mix the chicken with the Harissa paste & oil & refrigerate this can be done they day before or 2 hours before hand
2. In a heavy bottom pan heat some oil & add the onion, gently fry until just translucent add the garlic, & ginger, & continue to fry
3. Add the dry spices & continue to fry over add the Chicken & cook until well coated in the spices
4. Add ¾ of the chicken stock (add the remainder during the cooking process if sauce starts to get to thicken)
5. Add the chopped tomatoes, apricots & dates, stir well bring to the boil & simmer until the sauce starts to thicken
6. Add the chickpeas & cook for a further 10-15 minutes
7. Check the seasoning & adjust accordingly

Top Tips - you can add honey to sweeten & if you like the sauce a little thicker you can add a little cornflour to thicken

8. While the chicken is cooking prepare the butternut squash cut each half into nice slices
9. Toss in the spices & oil season with salt & Pepper & roast in the oven until tender
10. Place the couscous in a bowl drizzle with oil add salt pepper, lemon juice & mix well
11. Add boiling water to cover about 1cm above the couscous cover with cling film & leave until the water is absorbed
12. Remove the film & stir to ensure the couscous is light & fluffy
13. In a shallow pan heat a little oil & sweat the red onion until it becomes translucent add the chilli, add the couscous & toss all together
14. Stir in the ground almond & the apricot season to taste. Place in a dish & sprinkle with the herbs and toasted almond
15. Place the lemon wedges & herbs into the chicken stew & place into a bowl
16. Arrange the roasted butternut squash on a dish & sprinkle with some chopped coriander
17. Mix together the yogurt, honey & pomegranate seeds & serve as a dressing on the side

Chef: Scott Maslen (Actor)

How Did You Get Involved with YDWD?

Scott was looking for ways of helping out during the Covid-19 Pandemic and through a mutual friend got involved cooking meals for our NHS Heroes through 'You Donate… We Deliver'. Hopefully through this crisis we've learnt how important the NHS is to us and how much we need to protect them so that they can protect us!!

We have two versions of Scott's Shepherds Pie (one meat, one veggie)

Dish: 'Scott's Shepherd's Pie' (Part 1 – Meat)

Ingredients:

For the filling
- 500g lamb mince
- 250g onions, diced
- 5g of thyme
- 125ml of lamb stock
- 2 tbsp ketchup
- 500g carrots, Sliced
- 125g of celery
- 125ml white wine
- 1 tbsp of Worcestershire Sauce
- salt & pepper

For the topping
- 500g potatoes
- Oil
- 120g butter
- 2 egg yolks
- salt & pepper

Directions:

1. Bring a pot of water to the boil & drop in the potatoes. Boil for 15 minutes or until the potatoes are tender. Drain, then add the butter
2. Mash the potatoes until all lumps are removed and set aside
3. Place the lamb in a large pot or casserole dish with a little oil and cook until nicely browned. Drain to remove any excess fat
4. Place the pot over a medium heat and add the white wine. Heat until reduced by half then add the vegetables
5. Cook until they are softened but retain their crunch
6. Add the stock and reduce until the meat has absorbed all the liquid. Add more stock if the pie mix is a little dry
7. Season with salt, pepper & thyme and stir in the ketchup & Worcestershire sauce
8. Mix the 2 egg yolks into the mash – this will give the mash topping a glossy finish – and then spoon into a piping bag
9. Pipe the mash on top of the pie filling until completely covered
10. Place the pot or dish into an oven set to 200°c/gas mark 6 for around 30 minutes or until golden brown & bubbling
11. Serve immediately

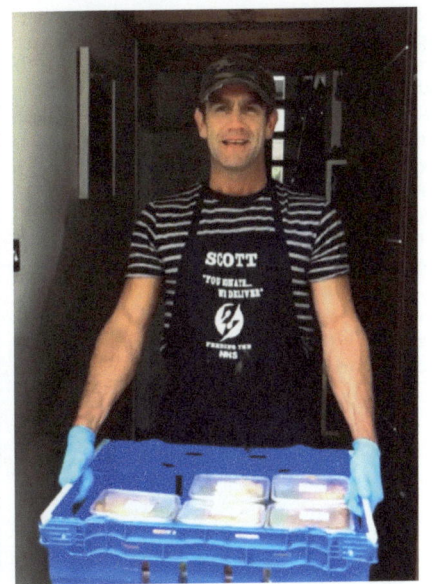

Chef: Scott Maslen

Dish: 'Scott's Shepherd's Pie' (Part 2 – Veggie)

Ingredients:

For the filling

400g tin green or puy lentils
1 leek, trimmed, finely chopped
1 large garlic clove, finely chopped
3 fresh sage leaves, roughly chopped
1 tbsp oil
1 tbsp Worcestershire Sauce
1 tbsp soy sauce
1 tsp caster sugar (optional)

2 Carrots, peeled & finely chopped
150g chestnut mushrooms, roughly chopped
3 fresh thyme sprigs, leaves only, finely chopped
400g tin chopped tomatoes
200ml vegetable stock
200ml red wine
1 tsp chilli flakes (optional)
salt & freshly ground black pepper

For the topping

500g sweet potatoes, peeled & cut into chunks
500g floury potatoes, peeled & cut into chunks
½ small cauliflower, separated into florets

knob of unsalted butter
salt & freshly ground black pepper
1 tbsp finely grated parmesan (optional)

Directions:

1. To make the filling, heat the oil in a frying pan over a medium heat. Add the leeks & fry for 4-5 minutes, or until beginning to soften
2. Add the carrots, mushrooms & garlic & continue to cook, stirring regularly, for 4-5 minutes
3. Add the sage, thyme, lentils, tomatoes, stock & red wine and stir together until well combined
4. Bring the mixture to the boil, then reduce the heat until it is simmering & continue to simmer for 18-20 minutes
5. Preheat the oven to 200˚c / 180 ˚c fan / gas mark 6
6. To make the topping, bring a large saucepan of water to the boil. Add the sweet potato & potato & boil for 10-12 minutes
7. Add the cauliflower & boil for a further 8-10 minutes, or until tender
8. Drain the vegetables well and return them to the pan
9. Add the butter, season well with salt & pepper, then mash until smooth. Set aside & keep warm
10. Stir in the Worcestershire sauce to the filling mixture along with the soy sauce, chilli flakes & sugar (if using)
11. Allow the sauce (which should have thickened during cooking) to simmer for a further 1-2 minutes
12. Add a little water if the mixture is too dry, simmer for longer if too watery. Season with salt & pepper
13. Transfer the filling mixture to an ovenproof baking dish, then spoon over the topping & spread into an even layer.

Top Tip – if you like a crispy topping, create peaks in the mash using a fork

14. Sprinkle over the parmesan (if using)
15. Bake the shepherd's pie in the oven for 18-20 minutes, or until the topping is golden brown & the filling is bubbling

Chef: Shabnam Russo

How Did You Get Involved with YDWD?

Mine is the story of an immigrant, told through food influenced by my journey from childhood in India, marriage in Venice & to my current life in London & Sardinia as I sought out my place in the world. My cooking helped carry me, providing both direction & comfort along the way. My food has always been about wanting people to accept me, but I'm also looking for acceptance from myself. In Hampstead Garden Suburb I am home.

I have a Bachelor's Degree in Hotel Administration from the Sheraton Group & won a scholarship at the prestigious management training program at the Taj group of Hotels, Palaces & Resorts in India , I moved to London soon after completion & pursued my passion in Hotels at the Four Seasons Hotel . I settled down in the Suburb with my family & set up my non-profit catering service as a hobby for friends & schools in the neighbourhood, New Year, Passover, Bar mitzvah's, Birthday parties, Celebration Cakes, Charity bake sales, social events & school fetes.

For a few years I have been cooking for a homeless shelter with the University College School children & it has given me immense satisfaction. My friend Katie Shmuel who I have catered for Rosh Hashanah last year recommended that I join the group 'You Donate, We Deliver' & I haven't looked back since. The NHS is the most amazing gift to our society & the most noble of all professions.

Debra Goodman who manages our Hub in HGS is phenomenal with her brilliant Chef daughter-in-law Christina Cramer. We can be creative with our cooking while she manages all the painstaking details of logistics, purchasing, health & safety labelling & delivery. Claudine Stone who I catered for in the past joined our team with her sister Louise De Groot Brick & we are a TEAM.

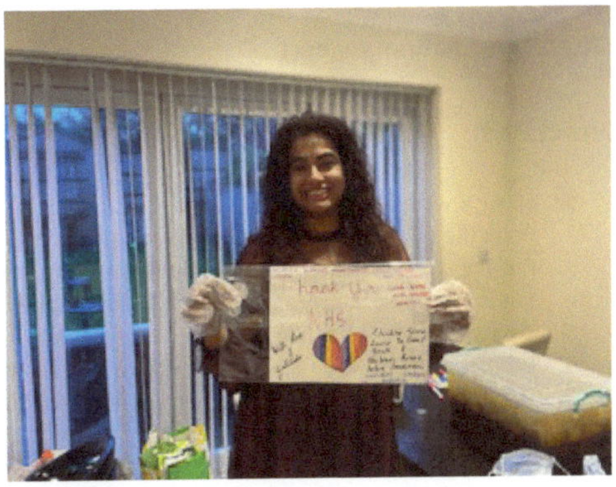

Dish: Lamb Koftas

With only 5 ingredients, these lean meatballs couldn't be easier to make!!

Ingredients:

500g lamb mince
2 tsp ground coriander
1 tbsp chopped mint
1 tsp ground cumin
2 fat garlic cloves, crushed
oil for brushing

Directions:

1. Mix together all the ingredients until well blended
2. Divide into eight balls, then roll each ball on a board with a cupped hand to turn them into ovals
3. Thread onto four metal skewers & brush with oil
4. To cook on a griddle: heat the pan until you can feel a good heat rising & cook for 3-4 mins each side
5. Don't turn until they are well sealed, or the meat will stick to the grill or pan
6. Season to taste & set aside
7. Serve the koftas with yogurt & spiced flat breads

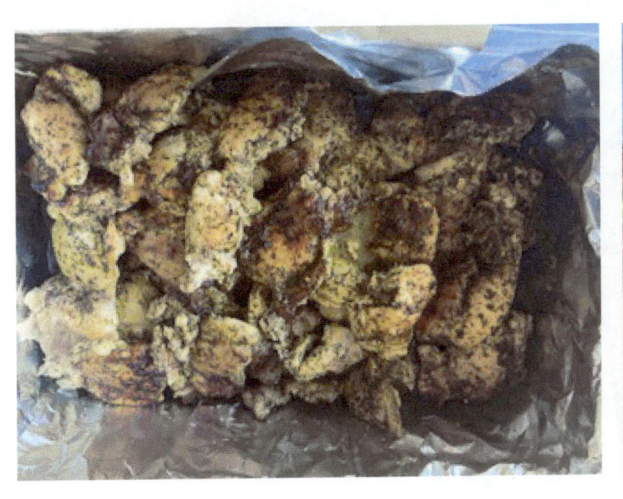

Chef: Shabnam Russo

Dish: Chicken Dhansak

This high-protein chicken dhansak curry with lentils is the perfect weekday supper to warm you up. With a GI of 50, this meal is high protein, low GI & provides 457 kcal per portion!!

Ingredients:

For the dish
low-calorie cooking spray
2 onions, finely chopped
20g ginger, finely grated
½ tsp hot chilli powder
600ml chicken stock, made with 1 chicken stock cube
100g dried red split lentils, rinsed & drained

2 garlic cloves, crushed
6-8 chicken thighs, boned, skinned & all visible fat removed
2 tsp garam masala
1 x 400g tin chopped tomatoes
2 bay leaves
200g wholegrain long grain rice

To serve
150g fat-free natural yoghurt

1 tbsp roughly chopped fresh coriander leaves

Directions:

1. Spray a wide-based saucepan or sauté pan with oil & place over a medium heat
2. Cook the onions for five minutes, stirring regularly, until softened & very lightly browned
3. Cut the chicken thighs in half & add to the pan. Cook for two minutes, turning occasionally
4. Stir in the garlic, ginger, garam masala & chilli powder & cook for a few seconds, stirring constantly
5. Tip the tomatoes into the pan & add the chicken stock, lentils & bay leaves
6. Bring to the boil, then cover loosely with a lid & simmer gently
7. Leave for 35 minutes, or until the chicken is tender & the lentils have completely broken down, stirring occasionally
8. Remove the lid for the last 10 minutes of cooking time, stirring regularly so the lentils don't stick
9. About 25 minutes before the curry is ready, cook the rice in plenty of boiling water until tender, then drain well
10. Season the curry to taste. Serve with the rice, topped with yoghurt & sprinkled with coriander

**Top Tips - If you don't fancy rice you could serve the curry with wholemeal flatbread, roti or salad.
Leftovers will keep in the fridge for a day or can be frozen**

Chef: Shabnam Russo

Dish: Cauliflower with Zahter

Ingredients:

2 large cauliflowers, trimmed & leaves discarded (1.3kg)
2 sprigs of sage (6g)
1½ tbsp tahini paste
3 tbsp olive oil (or 60ml, if using oregano instead of the zahter)
1 tbsp cider vinegar
3 tbsp zahter, drained from its oil (or 3 tbsp of picked oregano leaves)
5g coriander, roughly chopped

70g unsalted butter
8 strips of finely shaved lemon skin
1 tbsp lemon juice
1 onion, finely chopped (170g)
1 tsp honey
20g baby capers, pat dried
Salt

(Editor's Note: Zahter is a wild Turkish herb from the same family as Oregano & Thyme)

Directions:

1. Preheat the oven to 190°C
2. Sit the cauliflowers upright on your chopping board & cut two thick slices out of the centre of each cauliflower
3. You want the four slices – or 'steaks' – to remain held together at the base & each be about 4 centimetres thick
4. You should have about 400 grams of trimmings
5. Break these into even-sized pieces (if making the mash) & set aside
6. Add all of the butter to a large frying pan (or ½ the butter to two medium frying pans) & place on a medium heat
7. Add the sage, lemon skin & ¾ teaspoon salt (or ½ in each pan, if using two)
8. Once the butter starts to foam, add the cauliflower steaks, turning them in the pan so that they get covered in salt & butter on both sides
9. Fry gently for about 8 minutes, until golden-brown underneath & then flip the steaks over
10. Fry for another 8 minutes, until nearly cooked, & then transfer to a parchment-lined tray
11. Bake for 10 minutes, until the cauliflower is cooked through. Keep somewhere warm until ready to serve.
12. If making the mash, fill a medium saucepan with plenty of salted water & place on a high heat
13. Once boiling, add the cauliflower trimmings & boil for 15 minutes, until the cauliflower is really soft
14. Drain & then place in a food processor with the tahini, lemon juice, 2 tablespoon of water & a 1/8th of salt
15. Blitz to combine, using a spatula to scrape down the sides of the bowl, & then keep somewhere warm until ready to serve
16. Add 1½ tablespoons of oil to a medium frying pan (or 2½ tablespoons, if you are using the oregano leaves) & place on a medium-high heat
17. Add the onion & fry for 8 minutes until soft & caramelised
18. Add the vinegar & honey, stir through for a minute & then add the zahter (or oregano), along with a pinch of salt
19. Remove from the heat & set aside
20. Add the remaining 1½ tablespoons of oil to a small saucepan & place on a high heat
21. Once hot, add the capers & fry for about a minute, until the capers have opened out & are crispy
22. Use a slotted spoon to remove from the oil & set aside on a kitchen paper-lined plate
23. Too serve:
    Spoon 2 tbsp of the cauliflower & tahini mash onto each plate & spread out into a thin layer, not much larger than the cauliflower steak
24. Place the cauliflower steaks on top & then spoon over the onion & zahter (or oregano) salsa
25. Finish with a sprinkle of the crispy capers, along with the coriander, & serve

Chef: Simone Krieger (Krieger's Kitchen)

How Did You Get Involved with YDWD?

After completing my Business Management degree in Brighton, I became a home furnishings buyer for Marks & Spencer, which I did for 7 years. I left in 2000 to start my family & retrained as a Nutrition & Weight Management Specialist, tapping into my passion for health & food. In 2010 I established my company, Krieger's Kitchen, & finally realised my vocational dream. I love working in the catering industry as every day is different, bringing with it new & exciting challenges. I thrive on meeting new people & working as part of an ever-growing team.

On March 17th myself & my family went into self-isolation. This two week 'downtime' gave me time to pause, reflect & see what was going on in the world through the medium of social media. It was a particularly frustrating time for me as I could see there was much need all around me for something, I'm really good at & passionate about – food! On the first morning post isolation, I ventured into the scary world of lockdown. By 8.45am I was up, showered, dressed & in the van on my way to Makro. I had no idea what I'd find in the store or how readily available ingredients would be, so I went without a shopping list (very unlike me…. I love a good list!). Once there I bought a selection of ingredients, I knew would complement store cupboard items I had back at home.

I returned home, sanitised the kitchen & anything I had bought (& myself from memory!) & got cooking. I made a batch of around 30 two-portion meals of beef & barley casserole & photographed it. I could not wait to post my pictures on Facebook & see who I could help. I had no idea what the uptake would be, or whether anyone at all would be interested – or whether I would be eating beef & barley stew for the next 30 days. I had a number of individuals contact me asking for me to deliver them some containers of food, & then someone tagged Sarah Laster on my post. Sarah asked if she could take some & I was delighted to say yes – thinking she was another individual in need of a hot meal. "How many would you like", I asked…" I'll take all of them" she replied. I genuinely had no idea who or what I was delivering to on that sunny Friday morning on 3rd April – incidentally my 50th birthday!

I arrived in Borehamwood to find Jackie busily portioning plastic containers filled with meals into boxes labelled up for the three NHS hospitals she was now proudly supplying. I had a conversation with Jackie who told me about the amazing work that she, her daughter Katie & Sarah were doing. I was hooked! "So how many meals do you need & how often?" I questioned. The answer was simple, they would take as many meals as I could provide as often as I could make them.

What started as 25 portions of beef & barley stew being blindly delivered to someone with either a really large family or 'healthy' appetite, has now grown to me delivering 2-3 times a week on average 500 portions of food. If I could do more I would. I cannot tell you how super-humbled & impressed I am with the dedication & hard work of the entire team at YDWD. It has truly been an honour to be part of the team & grow with them as their project has expanded so massively over the weeks.

The Recipes: I'm giving you three recipes that I've been making week on week. They're all filling, nutritionally balanced (ish!) & delicious. I wanted to create at least a couple of dishes that would help NHS staff feel like they were having a bit of a treat. So quite a few of my recipes that I've been doing are based on restaurant/take-away favourites. The others are all homely-cooking style dishes such as pasta Bolognese, minestrone soup & so on, hoping to appeal to someone who might miss the comfort of home cooked dinners whilst they're out working long shifts.

Chef: Simone Krieger

Dish: Sticky Sesame Chicken – Serves 4

Ingredients:

For the chicken

5 tbsp vegetable oil
3 tbsp cornflour
½ tsp salt
½ tsp garlic salt
3 chicken breasts, cut into one-inch cubes

2 eggs, lightly beaten
10 tbsp plain flour
½ tsp ground black pepper
2 tsp paprika
2 tbsp sesame seeds

For the sauce

1 tbsp sesame oil
1 tbsp Chinese rice vinegar
2 tbsp sweet chilli sauce
2 tbsp brown sugar

2 cloves garlic
2 tbsp honey
3 tbsp ketchup
4 tbsp light soy sauce

Directions:

1. Heat the oil in a wok or large saucepan until piping hot
2. Whilst the oil is heating, place the egg in a shallow bowl & the cornflour in another shallow bowl
3. In a third bowl, mix the plain flour, salt, pepper, garlic salt & paprika
4. Dredge the chicken cubes in the cornflour, then dip into the beaten egg ensuring it's completely covered
5. Finally coat the chicken pieces in the seasoned flour
6. Add to the wok in small batches & fry until crispy. Remove & place to drain on kitchen roll or parchment
7. Add all of the sauce ingredients to the hot wok without the chicken pieces & bubble on a high heat
8. When the sauce thickens & reduces by around a third (this should take around 3-4 min) add the chicken pieces back to the wok
9. Stir through to ensure it's all coated. Cook for 1-2 minutes to ensure all the chicken pieces are cooked through thoroughly
10. Serve with rice or noodles topped with sesame seeds

Top Tips - For a really tasty vegetarian alternative, use tofu which has been well dried out by weighting down on top of kitchen rolls to absorb moisture.
Add half a teaspoon of garlic powder to the cornflour that's used to coat the chicken before frying

Chef: Simone Krieger

Dish: Genovese Penne with Roasted Vegetables – Serves 4

Ingredients:

2 courgettes, sliced into rounds
1 red onion, thickly sliced into about 8 slices
Handful of closed cup mushrooms, cleaned
1 tbsp olive oil
½ tbsp balsamic vinegar
½ tbsp toasted pine nuts – optional

2 peppers (any colour), cubed into 1 inch pieces
Handful of cherry tomatoes
1 small aubergine, cubed into half-inch pieces
1 level tsp sugar
½ jar of pesto
1 level tbsp crème fraiche

Directions:

1. Preheat oven to 190°C
2. Make pasta according to pack instructions
3. Meanwhile, prepare all the vegetables & put in a roasting dish with most of the olive oil, & all the balsamic vinegar & sugar
4. Season generously with salt & black pepper & bake in the oven until softened, but still slightly al dente
5. Drain the pasta & coat well with pesto & crème fraiche. Stir the pine nuts into the pasta & season well with salt & pepper
6. Serve either topped with the roasted vegetables or stir the vegetables through the pasta. Both ways make a tasty & balanced meal

Top Tip - The vegetables can be roasted a few hours in advance & kept warm or at room temperature

Chef: Simone Krieger

Dish: Sweet & Sour Chicken – Serves 6 (Ed. 4 in our house!!)

Ingredients:

For the chicken
1 small pineapple (or tinned if prefer)
4 tbsp sunflower oil
2 red peppers, deseeded & chopped into 2cm pieces
2 green peppers, deseeded & chopped into 2cm pieces

4 boneless, skinless chicken breasts
2 onions, roughly chopped
2 tbsp cornflour
6 spring onions, thinly sliced on the diagonal

For the sauce
2 tbsp cornflour
3 garlic cloves, crushed
2 tbsp dark soy sauce
4 tbsp soft light brown sugar
1-2 tsp dried chilli flakes

600ml pineapple juice
50g root ginger, peeled & finely grated
4 tbsp white wine vinegar
6 tbsp tomato ketchup

Directions:

1. To make the sauce, place the cornflour in a bowl & stir in 4 tbsp of the pineapple juice to make a paste. Put to one side
2. In a separate bowl combine the rest of the ingredients for the sauce
3. Peel & core the pineapple & cut into small chunks similar in size to the peppers. Cut the chicken breasts into one-inch cubes
4. Heat the oil in a large non-stick wok or skillet & add the onions & peppers. Stir-fry for 4 minutes on a high heat
5. Coat the chicken pieces in the cornflour ensuring each piece is well coated
6. Add the chicken to the pan & continue to stir-fry until the chicken is lightly coloured on all sides

Top Tip - Work in small batches if your wok is small

7. Add the pineapple chunks & the sauce to the pan & bring to a simmer over a medium heat
8. Cook until the chicken is cooked through & the pineapple is hot. This should take around 5-8 mins
9. Finally stir in the cornflour paste & cook for another minute or so until the sauce is thick & glossy
10. Stir well to ensure all the chicken & vegetables are well coated
11. Serve with rice or noodles sprinkled with thinly sliced spring onions

Top Tip - For a really tasty vegetarian alternative, use tofu which has been well dried out by weighting down on top of kitchen rolls to absorb moisture

Chef: Simone Krieger

Dish: Chicken Shawarma

Ingredients:

For the chicken

8 boneless, skinless chicken thighs
20g mild curry powder
100 ml olive oil
½ tsp pomegranate molasses
2 brown onions
Good handful finely chopped parsley & mint to serve

40g ras-el-hanout spice mix
1 tsp garam masala spice mix
1 lemon
2 small cloves garlic
Salt & pepper

For the tahini yoghurt

1 cup plain yoghurt
1 garlic clove, crushed
Salt to taste

1 tbsp tahini paste
½ lemon, zest & juice

Directions:

1. Mix all the marinade ingredients in a zip-lock back or flat dish.
2. Add the chicken into the marinade & give it a good 'massage'. Leave to infuse in the fridge for 6-12 hours
3. Preheat the oven to 200˚C. Finely slice the onions into 'half-moons' & place in the bottom of a roasting dish
4. Place the chicken on top of the onions & roast for 30-40 minutes – until the chicken thighs start to brown & are just cooked through
5. Remove chicken from the dish, & slice into thin slices
6. Remove the onions, & place in a preheated frying pan or skillet, on a high heat, to caramelise. This will take around 15 minutes
7. Meanwhile put the chicken back into oven, uncovered, to crisp up
8. After 5 minutes, turn the chicken pieces to bring the ones from the bottom of the dish to the top. Cook for a further 5 minutes
9. Whilst the chicken is cooking make the tahini yoghurt by mixing all the ingredients together
10. To serve, top the shawarma with the caramelised onion & serve with the tahini sauce either drizzled over the meat or on the side
11. Sprinkle generously with chopped herbs & enjoy with a fresh chopped salad, jewelled couscous or simply in a pitta with salad & chips!

Top Tip - For a vegetarian alternative, use cauliflower. Cook it whole for around 40 minutes, depending on the size of the cauliflower. It should retain its shape but be tender enough to slice. A sharp knife should easily go through the stalk as a test. Slice into 'steaks' to serve drizzled with tahini yoghurt & sprinkled with herbs.

Chef: Tanya Rosenthal

How Did You Get Involved with YDWD?

I saw Vicky Baruch post something on Facebook that she needed some sweet treats at the beginning of lockdown, so I got involved then & made some brownies. Since then I've been making hot meals & treats. I thought it would be good to get the kids involved, however the 18 & 16-year-old are usually still in bed when the chaos in the kitchen is created!! Lola who is 11 likes to help & husband Rob is happy to schlep.

Nice to feel I'm doing my little bit to help the amazing brave NHS staff x

Dish: Spinach Chickpea & Potato Curry

Ingredients:

1 onion, chopped
ginger a thumb-sized piece, chopped
1 tbsp vegetable oil
1 tsp ground coriander
1 x 400g tin chopped tomatoes
1 x 400g tin chickpeas, drained & rinsed
½ lemon, juiced
naans to serve

3 garlic cloves, chopped
1 green chilli, chopped
1 tsp ground cumin
1 tsp ground turmeric
400g Charlotte potatoes, cut into chunks
100g spinach, chopped
1 tsp garam masala

Directions:

1. Put the onion, garlic, ginger, chilli & 3 tbsp of water into a blender or food processor, & whizz until completely smooth
2. Heat the vegetable oil in a large, deep, non-stick frying pan, carefully add the onion purée & cook for 10 minutes until reduced & golden
3. Add the spices & cook for 2 minutes, then tip in the chopped tomatoes & bring to a simmer
4. Season & add the potatoes & chickpeas along with ½ a tin of water & simmer for 30 minutes
5. When the sauce has thickened & the potatoes have cooked through add the spinach & cook for a few minutes to wilt
6. Stir in the lemon juice & garam masala, & serve with naans

Chef: Tanya Rosenthal

Dish: Roasted Vegetables with Halloumi, Couscous & Chickpeas

Ingredients:

4 x colourful mixed peppers
3 x red onions
Approx. 15 colourful cherry tomatoes
1 x can of chickpeas
Olive oil
lemon

4 x large courgettes
3 x cloves of garlic
2 x 250 g of Halloumi
Couscous (I used pearl 250g & duchy organic 500g)
Cumin seeds
Salt & pepper to taste

Directions:

1. Cut all your veg up & layout on a large lined backing tray

Top Tip - Don't add the cherry tomatoes yet or Halloumi

2. Drizzle generous amount of olive oil & roast for about 20 mins, keeping an eye & moving the veg around so they get cooked evenly
3. Cut your cherry tomatoes in half's & throw them in & add drained chickpeas
4. Thinly slice the halloumi. Remove tray & add Halloumi & spread evenly. Sprinkle the dry cumin seeds on it
5. Cook for another 20 mins occasionally tossing veg & turn Halloumi
6. Cook the couscous.

Top Tip – Put the couscous in a bowl, with a spoonful of veg stock, cover with boiled water & top with a large plate & leave for 5-8 mins. Then fluff it up

7. Combine veg & couscous & serve

Chef: Tanya Rosenthal

Dish: Oat Choc Chip Cookies (They must be healthy; they have oats on them!!)

These are really easy to make & my 11 year old Lola now does them for me!!

Ingredients:

100g soft unsalted butter
1 medium egg
100g rolled jumbo oats
100g Cadbury dairy milk or any other milk choc chopped

100g light soft brown sugar
1 tsp vanilla Essenes
100g self-raising flour

Directions:

1. Preheat oven to 180°C. Grease 2 large sheets or line
2. In a large bowl, Beat the butter & sugar together until light & fluffy & then add egg & vanilla
3. Add the oats & sieved flour & fold in chocolate
4. Place spoonsful of the mixture evenly spaced on the sheet as they will spread out
5. Flatten with a fork
6. Bake for 10-15 mins. Cool on a wire rack

Chef: Tanya Rosenthal

Dish: 'Pret' Choc Chip Cookies (Ed. Shhhh Don't tell Pret!!) – Serves 8

Suitable for vegetarians

Ingredients:

110g Unsalted Butter
85g Light Brown Sugar
190g Self-Raising Flour
120g Large Dark Chocolate Buttons

170g Caster Sugar
1 Whole Egg
3g Salt

Directions:

1. Preheat the oven to 180°C. Melt the butter in a saucepan or microwave, until just melted (but not hot)
2. Using a stand mixer or electric beaters, beat the butter with the caster & brown sugars until well combined
3. Add the egg & beat on low speed until just incorporated – 10-15 seconds or so. Don't overbeat as this will result in a firm dough
4. Add the flour & salt. Mix until a smooth dough forms – again, be careful not to overmix!
5. Add the chocolate buttons to the dough & combine with your hands
6. For a good distribution of chocolate, don't be afraid to break up some of the buttons into pieces or chop them slightly beforehand
7. Scoop out 8 balls of dough & place on a non-stick or lined baking tray
8. Make sure there is plenty space between them as the dough will spread out in the oven
9. Press them down lightly with your palm to flatten them out a little & bake for 10-12 minutes until the cookies look puffed up & golden
10. Let the cookies cool on the pan for around 30 minutes as they will settle & sink into a dense buttery cookie

Top Tip – Best enjoyed warm (or place in an airtight container & eat within 3 days – Ed. Not sure they would last 3 days in my house!!!)

Chef: Victoria Prever (Food Editor – Jewish Chronicle)

How Did You Get Involved with YDWD?

I'm the food editor at the Jewish Chronicle, & a trained chef. I live in St Albans with my husband (who is working through this pandemic as presenting a BBC breakfast show in Oxford) & our two children aged nine & 11.

Katie Icklow's daughter is at school with my son. She called me at the end of March to see if I might be able to help cook for 'You Donate... We Deliver' as she knew my background. I was happy to send her 40 portions of curry & rice.

I wanted to do more, so agreed with my neighbour, Lisa Quait, that we would set up a 'hub' for St Albans. It grew fast, & within a couple of weeks we were sending more than 400 meals a week to them plus loads of bakes. I cook meals every other week & bake too. Even though I'm also working, & helping my children keep up with their schoolwork, it feels important to be helping with what can only be compared with a 'war effort'.

It has been great to meet lots of local people — the camaraderie has been amazing.

Dish: Quinoa, Bulgur Wheat, Cherry Tomato & Herb Salad with Tuna (Serves 4)

Ingredients:

1 tbsp Marigold vegetable bouillon (or vegetable stock powder)
90ml olive oil
Salt & black pepper
2 red onions, sliced into thin 'half-moons'
20g coriander leaves & stalk, roughly chopped
1 lemon (zest & juice)

250g white & red quinoa with bulgur wheat
2 tsp ras-el-hanout
300g cherry tomatoes
50g sultanas
20g mint leaves, roughly chopped
1 x 200g tin of tuna in olive oil, drained

Directions:

1. Bring a pan of water to the boil & add the vegetable stock powder
2. Pour in the quinoa/bulgur wheat mix & simmer cook for 12 mins — until the bulgur wheat is al dente & the quinoa seeds just burst
3. Drain, drizzle with 2 tablespoons of oil, & sprinkle with 1 teaspoon ras-el-hanout, ¾ teaspoon of salt, & plenty of pepper. Stir well to coat
4. Put 1 tablespoon of oil into a large frying pan & place over high heat
5. Once hot, add the tomatoes & fry for 3 to 4 minutes, stirring a few times, until they start to brown & split open
6. Pour into a bowl & sprinkle with a pinch of salt. Set aside
7. Wipe the pan clean, then add the remainder of the oil & return to medium-high heat
8. Add the onions, the remaining 1 teaspoon of ras-el-hanout, & a large pinch of salt
9. Fry 10 to 12 minutes — you will need to stir them frequently — until dark golden brown & soft
10. Remove from the heat, stir in the sultanas & leave to cool
11. Once the grains are a bit cooler, put them in a large bowl & add the onion & sultana mix
12. Stir, then add the drained tuna, herbs, lemon zest, lemon juice, ¼ teaspoon salt, & a generous grind of pepper & mix gently
13. Transfer to a serving platter, top with the tomatoes, & serve

Drawn by Olivia Benezra, age 12

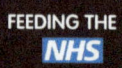

"YOU DONATE... WE DELIVER"   FEEDING THE NHS

"YOU DONATE... WE DELIVER"

FEEDING THE NHS

Lightning Source UK Ltd.
Milton Keynes UK
UKHW051610310720
367455UK00005B/32